HOW CAN I FIND GOD?

The

Westminster Books

Edited by
ARCHDEACON STORR
and
PRINCIPAL SYDNEY CAVE

HOW CAN I FIND GOD?

by

LESLIE D. WEATHERHEAD, M.A.

Author of :

*His Life and Ours, The Transforming Friendship,
Jesus and Ourselves, The Afterworld of the Poets,
After Death, Psychology in Service of the Soul, The
Mastery of Sex through Psychology and Religion, etc.*

LONDON
HODDER & STOUGHTON, LIMITED

First printed . . . *September, 1933*
Reprinted . . . . *October, 1933*

*Made and Printed in Great Britain for Hodder & Stoughton, Limited,
by C. Tinling & Co., Ltd., Liverpool, London and Prescot.*

THIS BOOK IS DEDICATED TO
MY SISTERS
MURIEL AND ALICE
IN GRATITUDE AND AFFECTION

THE WESTMINSTER BOOKS
EDITORS' PREFACE

THE general name " THE WESTMINSTER
BOOKS " has been given to this series
of volumes because the original proposal for such a series was made at
a small Committee which met under the
shadow of Westminster Abbey. It will
be noticed that each volume in the series
has a title in the form of a question (" Is
Sin Our Fault ? " " Do Dead Men Live
Again ? " and so on). There is a reason
for this. We live in a time when many
things are being questioned, and notably
religious beliefs and traditional theological
dogmas. The volumes in this series deal
with some of these questions of ethics
and religion which are arousing interest
or causing perplexity to-day in the minds
of many. They are not academic problems which are here discussed, but living
problems, the kind of problems which
men come up against every day as they
move about in a world flooded with
new knowledge in every department of

enquiry. This age, and especially perhaps the younger generation in this age,
wants to know what it can really believe
about God, the soul, immortality, moral
standards and the like, in face of all
that is being said by natural science,
psychology, comparative religion and
Biblical criticism. It is hoped that these
books may do something to meet this
need. They are written as far as possible
without technical language ; they endeavour to look facts fairly in the face,
and to shirk no difficulties. The writers
belong both to the Church of England
and the Free Churches. The series
therefore is not the product of any
narrow school of thought. The editors
have left each author free to state his
own opinion, and accept no responsibility for the views expressed. Their
work has been mainly that of selecting
the authors and securing, so far as is
possible, that their contributions do not
overlap. It is their confident hope that
the series will command a wide attention
and be of real help to many in their search
for truth.

VERNON F. STORR.
SYDNEY CAVE.

CONTENTS

CONTENTS

PROLOGUE
DO WE REALLY WANT
TO FIND HIM ?

DO WE REALLY WANT
TO FIND HIM ?

DOWN through the centuries from one of the oldest dramas in the Bible, perhaps *the* oldest, comes that wistful cry of Job, " Oh that I knew where I might find Him ! " ; and the cry is taken up by modern writers. G. K. Chesterton sings :

> So with the wan, waste grasses on my spear,
> I ride forever seeking after God.
> My hair grows whiter than my thistle plume
> And all my limbs are loose ; but in my eyes
> The star of an unconquerable praise ;
> For in my soul one hope for ever sings,
> That at the next white corner of the road
> My eyes may look on Him.

In the main, those who complain that they cannot find God—who say that prayer is unreal, that it seems like talking to nobody, that they never feel anyone is there, that their prayer lacks reality, and that the experiences they read and hear concerning others never happen to them—are perfectly sincere in their quest for God; but since God is what He is, the thing that is hindering them is on their side, not on God's, though exactly what that hindrance is may not be discernible by them, standing just where they are standing at present. For, though we ask the question, "How can I find God?" a truer way of putting the question would be, "How can I put myself in the way of being found by Him?" If God is what Jesus taught, then the One who was likened by Jesus to a shepherd seeking his sheep on the mountains, "until he find it," and to a woman seeking a coin, "until she find it," is searching for us with a steadfastness of purpose that puts to shame our little quest, with its hot and sometimes tearful resentments at ill-success. God, if He be our loving Father, definitely feels a sense of incompleteness if we are not at home in Him and with Him.

14

God, being what He is, is far more anxious to find us than we have ever been to find Him, and He will never rest until He brings us home.

There is therefore a preliminary question, " Do we really want to find Him ? "—since it is logical to argue that, if God is seeking us, and we, with our whole heart, are seeking Him, we shall be found by Him at once and brought into that delicious relationship of being at home in our Father's world, which accounts for so much of the joy, serenity, and strength manifested in the life of Jesus.

" With our whole heart "—these are the words which contain the difficulty, and that is perhaps the reason why, for some of us at any rate, the quest for God seems barren and fruitless and God seems to have withdrawn Himself to a distant heaven. " If *with all your hearts* ye truly seek Me ye shall ever surely find Me." The truth is that we want Him and do not want Him, and there is

Deut 4²⁹

a conflict in our minds which defeats our quest and spoils our experience. Let us look at this conflict very closely.

We want Him. We have read some of the lives of the saints; and when we have made every allowance for the fact that some of them were undoubtedly neurotics, some were mystics, some were visionaries, and it may be said that their outlook on life was abnormal, yet many of them had a sense of the presence of God which was convincing to them and in every way satisfying; and we cannot dismiss the experience of the saints in all ages as mental disease, for it is more wholesome, satisfying and attractive than our health. We have had our little moments when a sense of presence has fallen upon us, but Brother Lawrence could truly say that he was as conscious of the presence of God when among the pots and pans of his kitchen as when he was on his knees before the Blessed Sacrament. Hymn-writers can use phrases which make us hunger for the experience

16

about which they write, and some of our friends tell us about experiences that we would give almost anything to have. These experiences of others make us truly long for God.

Then there are times of loneliness and need and sorrow, when no human friend can enter into our heart, and when our whole nature cries out for the comfort and strength which it believes God can bring. No preacher who is really in touch with people, and who has achieved any skill in the art of reading faces, could look down from a pulpit without being deeply impressed by the kind of spiritual hunger which people's faces express. And if he is in sympathy at all he is bound to be deeply moved by the amazing courage of men and women. Many of them are carrying heavy burdens and going through the darkest valleys. Some are troubled as to how in the world they are going to make both ends meet. Some are in deep distress over husband or wife or child.

B

Some are bearing a loneliness which is almost a physical pain. Yet, for the most part, men and women put on a bright face and bear their troubles in an uncomplaining silence ; and only when they relax, as they do in Church, can it be seen that some are almost at the end of their strength—tired in heart and brain and body, wondering if they will really get through another week, and almost desperate to find God. So much so that the preacher, if they only knew it, is almost as desperate, with a longing to give them the sense of God which has come to himself, which he knows would buoy up their spirits, steady their nerves, be a tonic to their minds, and send them forth with radiant face and renewed strength, feeling that because God was with them, nothing in heaven or earth or hell could down them. Yes, there is not the slightest doubt that we want God. We simply must have Him or break down.

But there is another side to the picture

and we must be brave enough to face both sides of our conflict. Many of us want God much as we want a hot-water bottle at night—a little temporary comfort, which would just bring us through a trying hour and then could be pushed away by other things within the self. We cannot play fast and loose with God like that. I have been reading, for the stiffening of my own spine, some of the experiences of God that men of olden days had. You will remember that if you touched the Ark in the days of the old Covenant, you were a dead man. If you touched the mountain in which, in terror and power, He was supposed to dwell, it was instant death. We must remember, when we talk so glibly about direct access to God, that only once a year after tremendous preparation and prolonged self-discipline did the High Priest enter into the Holy of Holies. We need to recover the Jewish sense of the majesty of God. " In the year that King Uzziah died I saw the Lord, high and lifted up, and His train filled the Temple, and one cried unto another and and said : ' Holy, Holy, Holy is the Lord of Hosts. The whole earth is full of His glory.' Then said I, ' Woe is me for I am undone, because I am a man of unclean lips.' "

God must not be thought of as a beneficent fairy godmother who, by the turning of a ring, can be brought to our aid to turn our dusty rubbish heaps into gold and our hovels into fairy palaces. Nor must we treat Him as a kind of Harrods at which we ask for things and then lose faith in the business because what we ask for is not sent up by dinner time. Nor must we bargain with Him as Jacob did : " If God will bless me and keep me in the way that I go and give me bread to eat and raiment to wear so that I come again to my father's house in peace, then shall the Lord be my God." We must, in a word, want Him with our whole mind, and want Him for His own sake, and not for what we can get out of

Him—not even the undoubtedly *good* things we want from Him.

As I said, there is the difficulty—" Want Him with our whole mind." We talk, too glibly sometimes, about the presence of God. If we were pure we might stand before Him and bear the glory of His presence. But if the splendour of His glory really did break upon us, if He answered the prayer we so often pray, " Show us Thy face," should we not be like those who called on the mountains to cover them and the hills to fall on them ? Should we not wrap the rags of our self-righteousness round us and run from Him ? For if we are going to face the question, " Do we really want to find Him ? " does the answer not depend on this very question—" Do I really love my sins, my compromises, my fears, better than Him ? " We want Him now, perhaps at the moment, or in some lonely desolate hour, or even, as in the case of many people, when they are bursting with health and good spirits ;

but in the hour when the pulses of noble-
ness are slow, when low temptations
possess us, when some unclean lust
sweeps through us like a burning fire,
or when we are so afraid of what people
would say or think if we stood out for
what we know to be right—in such
moments, do we really want Him ? Or
do we not want far more the very things
He hates ?

So we find ourselves in the grip of
this terrible conflict. We want Him
and we do not want Him. We want
His way and we want our own way.
We want to be made clean, but there is
still a hunger for the husks that the
swine eat. We want to do His will,
but our will chokes our desire. We
would see His Kingdom come, but we
give our vote in another direction. We
would follow Christ, but we do not
want to do so openly lest our friends
should think we are queer. We need
forgiveness, but are too proud to let God
forgive us. So we are held in the grip

22

of our conflict and we are trying to live in two worlds.

Now that attempt to live in two worlds at once spoils the chance of our full experience of God and wrecks the life of our soul. You cannot be happy in either world if you are trying to live in both. If you are living wholly in God's world, wanting only Him, seeking with your whole strength His way, then life has a radiant, exultant experience. Everything speaks to you of God and nothing has power to drag you down because it cannot spoil your relationship. If you are living wholly in the world of sense and self in which the soul is lulled to sleep, you have at any rate such happiness as the entirely selfish life can bring. But many of us, between two worlds, settle down to what we call a compromise, but which is a dangerous psychological conflict which takes full toll of our nervous poise. We will serve in His Church, support its finances, argue for its intellectual position, or hide in any other dug-out which happens to be in our section of the line. We tell ourselves that the experiences of others are not for us. The real truth is that consciously or unconsciously we are evading God. We *must* be doing so if He seeks us and yet we are not found of Him.

I believe God has an experience for us which is greater and more splendid than anything we have ever known. I believe He throws open the gates of a new world to us which is sheer wonder and delight. I believe we can live in a world where His presence is the very atmosphere we breathe and where almost everything we touch reminds us of Him; but I believe we must be ready to give up our sins and fears and compromises, and go with Him as He calls us. At first it will be a discipline, but we must let Him burn sin and self out of us. The glory of His presence will be surgical at first, but Christ and all the saints and apostles beckon us on and their lives give a triumphant " Yes " to the question, " Is

24

it really worth it?" And when we ask the question, "How can I find God?" we must answer these other questions first—"Do I really want to find Him? Am I prepared to leave the things that, like a dreadful cloud, come in between my soul and Him?"

We must desire Him more than we desire anything else in the world; and if He puts His finger on this and that and says, "These things must go first," He will give us the courage to cut them out entirely. He will help us to pray sincerely, "What wilt Thou have me to do?" and then give us grace, so that whatsoever He says unto us we may do it.

PART I
ARE WE HIDING FROM HIM?

I
IN REFUSING
TO REPENT ?

S T. MARK, in the earliest of the four gospels, in the gospel in which we are most likely to find the actual words of Jesus, quotes Jesus as opening His ministry with the words, " Repent ye and believe in the gospel." Or, in our language, [1] " Change your way of looking at life and believe in the good news " (Mark i, 15).

Most of us have in our minds already the thought that repentance on our part is the first condition in all those who seek God, but they are by no means clear as to what repentance means nor how one goes about it. It is obviously impossible to sit down and say, " Go to, I will now repent." Yet we feel the point is of great importance and Jesus' emphasis

[1] *See* Archbishop Temple in *Christian Faith and Life.* In this section I am especially indebted to the various writings of Dr. Temple and Dr. Clow.

31

deepens this impression. We shall discuss these two problems in this section.

It is often the easiest way to see a thing if we can clear from the mind some misapprehensions.

(*a*) Repentance is not remorse, though the former may contain the latter. But remorse, as such, has no power in it to set us on the right road. It is a mental torture often containing elements of self-loathing, but leading rather to utter despair than to a new way of looking at life. People in remorse tend to excess or even to suicide. They do not feel it to be essentially a healthy state of mind. In repentance, however searching, upsetting, and even distressing, the soul feels that it is good to repent.

(*b*) Repentance is not merely self-reproach. A man often feels a fool in some situation and reproaches himself. He is chafed and humiliated, but his emotion is still selfish. It is often a subtle form of self-pity. It has no power or cleansing about it.

32

(*c*) Repentance is not fear of consequences. Often the spirit is stabbed by thoughts of what might happen if one were found out. The mind during some sleepless night makes terrifying phantasies of the results of exposure ; of what we should feel if our friends knew what we were really like. Such fear may make a temporary difference to our way of living, but it has insufficient power to change life's direction ; and with this alone at work we are soon back in the old ways, perhaps taking, however, greater pains to prevent exposure.

(*d*) Repentance is not the mere sense of sin. The conscience is well able to tell us, " This is right," " That is wrong," but it has little power to change the current of our lives. A saying of Butler is relevant here : " Had the conscience the power as it has the authority, it would absolutely govern the world."

(*e*) Repentance is not to be measured by feeling. Often deep feeling plays a part in a true repentance, but you can have

33

c

a true repentance without deep emotion and you can have a deep emotion without true repentance. When I lived in Manchester I gladly accepted an invitation to take part in a Mission at a neighbourng church. Every night for a week the church was thronged and the missioner pleaded with people to come into an enquiry room and be converted. The emotional, tense atmosphere simply swept people in, and the average number per night of people who professed conversion was two hundred. The missioner instructed them to attend the church or chapel nearest them, but although my church was only two hundred yards away, out of over a thousand converts, we only welcomed two, and other ministers in the neighbourhood reported similarly disappointing results. From the window where I write these words I can see the flowers in my garden. They are moving in response to the cool evening breeze. After a sultry August day, in fancy I imagine them grateful for this cool breeze, responding to it as they bow before it out there in the dusk. But they will all be there in the morning. They will not have begun a new way of life. Again and again we have responded emotionally to this influence or that voice, but the next morning, the next month, the next year finds us just where we were. We were emotionally moved. But we did not repent. We did not change our way of looking at life.

(f) Repentance is not merely a negative attitude. We used to sing:

> Repentance is to leave
> The things we loved before,
> And show for them we grieve,
> By doing them no more.

But this is not nearly enough. Repentance is changing your way of looking at life. It is steering under a new star and bringing the whole life into subjection. It is not only giving up this sin and that. It is a new, positive change of direction which affects the whole of life, the use of

our time, our money, our leisure, our
talents, the way we do trivial things and
the way we react to other people. It is
to think again ; often it is a complete
volte-face. The happy soul has found the
only star to steer by which will bring it
where, in its best moments, it most wants
to be.

Thus repentance, thought of so often
as an experience full of tears, is primarily
marked by a sense of deep joy. Repentance is often mixed with elements of
remorse, fear, a sense of sin, and self-
reproach and for this reason a sense of
holy awe invades the spirit and the
tears of the penitent are usual. But
these things are the concomitants of
repentance rather than the thing itself.
The essence of repentance should be
manifested by a joy in which, Jesus tells
us, the very angels of heaven share. [1]

Indeed, if a man is bankrupt and
suddenly finds a new source of untapped
revenue for the costly business of living,

Luke xv, 10.

shall he not rejoice? If a man is lost in a jungle where, all night, low branches whip his face and dank undergrowth trips his feet; if thunder crashes overhead, lightning flashes among the trees, rain lashes his face relentlessly; if he finds no way through and is almost in despair— and this is no exaggeration of the plight in which many feel themselves to be just now—and suddenly the dawn breaks and there is a path that leads him out of the jungle on to a highroad on which any wayfaring man may find the way home, shall he not rejoice? If a man has lost his sense of right values, setting his heart on things worthless, and letting go the things that matter most, blinded by the trick the world has of confusing what he wants with what he needs, and then through some inner enlightenment he *sees* into the heart of things and *knows* the things that belong to his peace, shall he not rejoice? Did not those to whom Jesus spoke, rejoice when they listened to Him and looked at the quiet radiance of

His glorious face; when they knew by an inner authority, which was not that of Scribes, that religion was not a dreary code of " Thou shalt nots," not a relationship of fear, not a finicking attention to ceremonial details, but a twofold attitude in which any man or woman could look up into the face of God and say, " My Father," and into the face of his fellow and say, " My brother, my sister " ? What good news ! " Change your way of looking at life," cried Jesus, " and believe the Good News."

What shall we say to the man who says, " I can't repent because I'm told to. I know I'm a sinner. I hate myself often, but at other times I like doing the things I do. I love them more than virtue. How can I be made to repent ? "

The glory of the gospel is that it never makes a demand without showing us how to fulfil it. If we had seen the face of Jesus when He uttered the words we have quoted so often, we should not have said " How can I be made to repent ? "

38

If we could realise what good news He does bring, the question would not arise. Perhaps if our imagination does not come to our aid two considerations will do so.

The first is that there *is* only one star to steer by which brings us where we want to be. The desires of the self do at times seem overwhelming. But if we indulge in them they bring us no real satisfaction, no ultimate peace. Life will only work in one way. It is the way Jesus trod and taught. In a sense it is a " steep path." We have to " strive " to enter in. But it is the only path that gets us anywhere. All others are marked, sooner or later, " No THOROUGHFARE." It is a deluded ease to go down a path if you have to turn back. The way of Christ is easiest in the long run. It is the only way *through* ; the only method that works. Of all the methods suggested to us in these days by which life can be lived, still His way stands out as the only way which has been tried and proved to work. The world is full of leaders, but none of them, save as they themselves follow Him, are leading us toward any place worth getting to. He is the Way. There are many false stars, even bright ones. But people find at last, even though it be after much irritation and when nerves and tempers are threadbare, that there is only one " bright and morning Star " which is the true star of human destiny. His quiet voice still says, " Ye will not come to Me that ye might have life." But when once we have seen God's way, when once we have had a vision of the new world Christ opens up, we shall never have peace, never be satisfied, till we are His.

All this is true of the world around us. Men are being driven to try the way of Christ because all other ways fail. In the matter of war, industrial relationships, labour disputes, methods of government we try all ways ; but we are slow to repent, to change our way of looking at life and believe the good news. It would help us to repent if we realised the failure of every other way save that of Christ.

The second thing we may say to the man who cannot repent is to ask him to consider what our failure costs God. If Jesus is a revelation of God then in His anguish we can see God's reaction to sin. When we see Christ in the Garden and on the Cross still loving men with a love that never counts the cost, but goes on in an unbroken love to the bitter end; when we realise that God loves us like that at this very moment, then there is no sin so dear that we will not give it up that we may become what His love could make us; what, when we look at the Cross, we want to be. One glance of real insight at the Crucified and our sinning pride and complacencies are down for ever.

But we must be honest with ourselves. Have we not sought for God, longed for an experience, shuddered with remorse and fear and self-reproach, called ourselves hard names, cried ourselves to sleep,

but never repented, never changed the
star under which we sailed, never changed
our direction? Have we not hidden
indeed from God under a stubborn
refusal to let Him interfere too deeply,
change our way of life too radically, put
His finger on our leprosy too remorse-
lessly? Have we not cushioned ourselves
with compromises, turned our eyes away
from His Cross, gone on our way drugging
our consciences with lies, pretending we
had a true experience of Him, or that it
was not for people with our temperament,
or that there was nothing more in Christianity than we had found already, or
that, anyway, we did not pretend to be
saints and so could cherish one or two
secret sins without feeling too bad about
it? In a word we are hiding from God,
we who pretend to be seeking Him, lest,
yielding to Him utterly, He should ask
us to become more than we dare to be.

II
IN INTELLECTUAL QUEST?

IN INTELLECTUAL QUEST ?

CONSIDERING further the way we hide from God though we are supposed to be seeking Him, we may note how easy it is to hide from Him in our intellectual quests.

The age in which we live is remarkable, from the religious point of view, for the sincerity of its intellectual quest. Youth, rightly I think, refuses to live for six days in a scientific world and pass, on the seventh, into a world of magic. All our young people nowadays are getting what might be called a scientific education. Many of them go to college or the university. There they are taught not to accept anything without adequate evidence. We cannot expect them to accept great truths on Sundays because they are embodied in a creed or written in the Bible or were believed by their grandfathers.

As an American writer says : " Six days in the week we live in an ordered world. On the seventh, we open the church door on a land of topsy-turvy, where axes float, dry sticks change to serpents, cities are let down out of the sky, angels stir the water of wells, be-devilled swine run violently into the sea. We say prayers for rain an hour after we have consulted a government bulletin to see whether we shall need an umbrella before we get home. We solemnly repeat, ' Maker of heaven and earth . . . descended into hell . . . sitteth on the right hand of God . . .' Yet all the while we know perfectly well that heaven is not ' up ' nor hell ' down ', that this universe was never ' made ' by anybody in any such sense as the ' apostles ' supposed, nor has it any such topographical relations as they assumed." [1]

It is one of the most healthy signs in modern religion that such situations as

[1] E. T. Brewster, *The Understanding of Religion*, p. 27. Quoted by H. E. Fosdick, *The Modern Use of the Bible* (S.C.M.), p. 53.

this are being met by honest intellectual quest. It is a sound instinct, if the word be allowed for the moment, that nothing should be received as the truth until it is seen to be true. Surely this is what Jesus Himself would have us do when He says that part of the first and greatest commandment is that we should love the Lord our God with all our mind.

At the same time that very intellectual quest, worthy as it is, can be a spiritual dug-out in which the soul hides from God.

I have attempted to show in another place[1] that quite frequently men hold back from allegiance to Christ on the ground that they do not understand Christianity. They don't hold back from riding in a motor-car because they are ignorant of the principle of the internal combustion engine. Quite honestly the difficulties in the way of a man who would find God are very rarely intellectual. It is not the Virgin Birth, or miracles, or

[1] *The Transforming Friendship* (The Epworth Press).

the divinity of Christ, or the Resurrection. It is more likely impurity, selfishness, or bad temper. But it is pleasant to call oneself scientific and let the soul believe that its quest is hindered by intellectual doubts. We may remember that Jesus never demanded intellectual assent to any proposition of the intellect before men became His disciples. He asked them to follow a way of life, not to subscribe to an intellectual creed, and any church is wrong which *demands* allegiance to a creed as a condition of membership. But it is so easy, when our courage is not quite equal to complete surrender to His way of life, to suppose that intellectual doubts are in the way.

In a similar if less serious way thousands of young people haunt " Swanwick " and similar group conferences every year. They discuss every aspect of the Christian life and every branch of theological thought. Many are frankly exhausted at the end of the week though the fellowship is certainly a fine and exhilarating thing. Their minds are packed with ideas, but one girl, a habituée of such conferences, spoke the thoughts of many hearts when she said, " I have hundreds of new ideas. What I want now is the courage to put a single one of them into operation in my life." Seeing that saved her from the dug-out of intellectual quest which stifles the life. But many do not see this, and it gives the soul the sense of being religious to talk about these things and discuss theological and even practical religious problems. It is astonishing how the real relation of the soul to God can be left, after much discussion, just where it was, or perhaps in a worse condition, since the mind is blinding itself to the very realities it sets out to discover. All preachers know that it is one thing to know a lot about God and another thing to be living in contact with Him. It is one thing to be able to answer all the questions people will ever ask about the problems of prayer. It is another thing to keep one's own prayer

49

D

life fresh and *real*. It is not difficult to let one's ideals go, arguing subconsciously, " I will make up for the loss of my own ideals by passionate defence of the faith." The discussion of theology is a very adequate defence of the soul from God. The conversation of the woman of Samaria with Jesus is relevant here. It is surely one of the most fascinating conversations in literature. One wonders why the woman was at the well at midday at all. In the East, as every one knows, water is drawn from the well in the early morning, and again, if necessary, in the evening. No one would choose midday in order to carry a heavy water pot to and from the village. Is it not because she fears the eyes and tongues of other women she would meet? Therefore, she finds in the blazing sunshine of noon a greater protection than she would find in the gathering shadows of evening. Then, to her dismay, she runs right into One whose eyes pierce to the centre of her being and in whose presence her soul seems naked and ashamed. I suppose there happened with her what would have happened with us if we had looked into the eyes of Jesus. All her defences were down in a few seconds. The dug-out of excuses and compromises crumbled over her head, and we may watch her evading, with her woman's wit, His direct challenge. It may be noticed that again and again she tries to change the subject, first with banter as to whether Jesus is greater than Jacob who gave the well; secondly, by deliberately misunderstanding Him about the "living water" about which He speaks; thirdly, she as much as says, " Do not let us talk about my husbands. Let us discuss where people ought to say their prayers." Jesus courteously and completely answers all her questions, but He inexorably comes back to the first thing to get right, her personal relationship with God, and He does it until He saves a soul. He will not allow her to take refuge in the dug-out of argument. He forces her to reality.

Some months ago, after preaching in a well-known London church, I received a letter from a young woman graduate, who appeared to be in great need. She has permitted me to quote her story. "I am in despair," she wrote, "and I would come up to Leeds if only you would help me." On a certain Thursday afternoon she came, and for one and a half hours we discussed evolution, immortality, the inspiration of the Bible; and after we had put out some of the flames of hell I leant over towards her and said, "You did not really come two hundred miles in the train to talk to me about hell-fire, did you? What is the real problem?" The girl looked at her wrist watch and said, "I am very sorry but I am afraid I shall have to go to catch my train," and the door closed behind her. On the Saturday evening, however, my telephone bell rang and the same voice came over the wire: "I could not go back to London, I stayed in Leeds. I am sorry I wasted your time.

Can I see you again?" She came round an hour later, and the real problem was disclosed: "How can I find Christ for myself?" I shall never forget that interview, because one had the curious sense that sometimes comes to one of watching Someone else direct an interview. I cannot remember a single word that I said to her. I was more conscious that Christ was there talking to that girl, than of the desk at which I sat. Her face lit up with an amazing radiance and she found the new world which Christ offers. It was the birth of a soul which had been sheltering from God in the dug-out of intellectual difficulties and arguments.

Again and again in one's psychological work the same fact emerges. I talked for hours with a young doctor, recently, who voiced some of the most bitter criticisms I have ever heard against religion and the Church. I was quite unsuccessful in helping him, but in the end he did admit that his criticism was the projection on to the Church of his own utter helplessness to deal with his own moral compromises. I can recall case after case of people who seek psychological help. Their nerves are wrong. They are sleepless. There is a tight feeling round their head. There is a pain at the base of the spine. They are irritable. They are ' fed-up.' They are thinking of doing away with themselves. (It is surprising how many people talk about this.) Yet again and again when one gets down to the bottom of their minds, one finds that prayer has been given up altogether or is a farce, that there is something they will not forgive, some sin they will not confess, some inward resentment, some hidden jealousy that eats away their peace, some defilement or unclean lust that spoils the poise of their spirit and gets between them and God. And they try to get out of it by worrying themselves into frenzies about intellectual questions that have nothing to do with their problems. Some of us who spend many hours helping people to straighten out their intellectual difficulties find that those difficulties are trenches in which men are hiding from God. Drive them from one and they take refuge in another. Finally it is generally discovered that there is only one religious difficulty. It is the difficulty of being religious, of surrendering to God and allowing Him to lead us where He will.

III
IN SERVICE
TO MEN ?

DEVELOPING our argument, we may note further how it is possible to hide from God in our service to men on His behalf. Some men say that they have found God through service to their fellows. We shall discuss this later. First, let us see that it may be a shelter in which the soul hides from God.

If this age is notable for its intellectual quest in religion it is as notable for its emphasis on service. In no other age were so many people engaged in service for their fellows. Never before were there so many magnificent enterprises with which people *could* identify themselves. But for some folk it is true to say that the very passion of their service is the measure of their compromise. If the unconscious motives of some minds were made conscious and then vocal we should hear many confess thus : " I can never be the man I wanted to be. I set out with high ideals, but they are beyond me. I've struggled for long against besetting sin. Now I give up the struggle as hopeless. But I'll throw myself into the service of God." Nor are we to disparage such service. It is excellent. And surely God honours it and receives it and uses it. But the first thing is not right, the personal relation between the soul and God.

We are all very much like little children before God. Without a violent effort of imagination I can think of two little boys in a family who sometimes quarrel. We will imagine the younger striking the older. His mother, being very wise, does not punish or rebuke, but her eyes are sad. The little chap is so anxious to get things right. He says, " Mummy, are there any errands you want running ? " and he will run her errands. With his own penny I have known him to buy her a pathetic little present. She will receive it, but her eyes do not regain their joy and peace. He will chatter, and the extent of his chatter is the measure of his own disharmony. At last his good angel tells him there is only one way. He flings himself into his mother's arms with some expression, however inadequate, of sorrow, " Oh, Mummy, forgive me." Then her eyes shine again. The whole world is a new place. With what verve he now runs her errands and with what new delight will she now receive his present and listen to his baby talk.

Is it not so with many of us ? We think we are serving God, but we are running His errands, doing Him service, subscribing to His Church, to avoid that adjustment of relations which calls for an utter surrender which we have never given. He who truly seeks God must learn this lesson : first the Father's arms, then the Father's errands. First the solving of our own moral conflicts, then our service to a hungry world. First our own sins and then our brother's needs.

First the beam in our own eye, then the smut in our brother's. There is all the difference in the world between service which is an expression of a relationship and service which is an attempt to evade a relationship.

Look for a moment at Saul of Tarsus. His experience on the way to Damascus was not, we feel, his first experience of Christ. He may have been present at the Crucifixion. He was certainly present at the stoning of Stephen, and in Stephen's eyes he saw something that disturbed him. What is the reason of the passionate service—to him, Church service—which he rendered immediately afterwards ? We all do things desperately and violently, when by doing them we hope to stifle some voice to which we do not want to listen. We will not give ourselves time to listen to it, and this is the explanation of Saul haling men and women to prison. His own mind is not easy. He is dimly aware that the first thing in religion is not right ; that he is not willing to have it right. He is stumbling along the trench that leads to the dug-out of service in which the soul hides from God. But on the way to Damascus the roof of the dug-out fell in. A light streamed from heaven which blinded his physical eyes but opened the eyes of his soul, so that for the first time he, who, like so many of us, had a name for being religious, really found God.

We must not disparage argument or service, or suppose that they are all motived in this way, but again and again both are symptoms of an evasion of that very experience we are said to be seeking.

If we look at both the intellectual quest and the emphasis on service in modern religion, it must be a cause of wonder that with all our Church organisations and the irrefutable intellectual basis of Christianity the world in her problems does not follow the way we advocate. When I ask myself what is the matter, I seem to see a castle on a hill called, " The

Castle of Life." Thousands are seeking entrance to it. For every man and woman one talks to, really wants to be able to manage this difficult business of living. Disabled lives, all around us, cry out to us to know if we can tell them the secret of the mastery of life. So the crowd surges in tumult round the gates of the castle, and a man, with grey face and sad expression, turns to you and says, " Do you know where the key may be found to the Castle of Life ? " and you say, " I have got it. Christianity is the key to life," and he looks at you incredulously and turns away. For, not without reason he argues that if you had it you would apply it. You would not be amongst the throng of seekers. You would be racing up the hill with radiant face and infectious gaiety, shouting, " Come with me, I have found it."

So the world looks at us rather wistfully. We say, " Christ is the key. We know the way." But having looked at us men pass on, and with a strange expression in their eyes; for what do they see?—our grey faces. We ask them to come to Church, press them to join our organisations, argue with them intellectually; but we are like men who claim to have a certain cure for some specific disease and who sometimes recommend it, yet the world can see the symptoms of the disease in their own faces. So it is that the unrest and problem of the world are the unrest and problem of our own hearts writ large. We have not got the first thing right for ourselves, and the way of Christ cannot be successfully advocated to the world by people who have not tried it themselves.

Look at the matter another way. Because we have not got the first thing right ourselves, we lose our faith in the Church's method. We need not disparage one thing in order to emphasise another. Let us welcome any measure that will help put the world right. The Act of Parliament, economic research, propaganda, and strongly supported resolu-

65

E

tions have their place, but these are not
the first work of the Church. The
Church's first work is to change men's
lives. This is a slow business, as Jesus
said it would be. Moreover, it is often
not dramatic or sudden or obvious in its
results. It is like the leaven spreading
slowly from cell to cell; an infection
passing from man to man as one loving
spirit sets another on fire. External
measures seem much more effective.
They look like what the world calls
" getting a move on," and so many church-
men put their faith in such measures.
But the difference is the difference between
locking up a lunatic, and curing his mental
disease. The first is dramatic, sudden,
effective, showy. The second is slow,
with little to see and with few crises.
External measures to make the world
better are like locking up the lunatic;
but no Act of Parliament, no economic
change, no resolution, will bring in the
golden age or cleanse the world. They
will only restrain the world. And many

are getting tired of them. We change Governments, but as Studdert Kennedy once said, we only take one lot of sinners out and put another lot in. We constantly change the scenery, but the plot is the same.

The Church's first work is the curing of the disease ; getting men into the right relationship with God. If I could bring a slum landlord, or the owner of a brothel, or the man who sweats people in his factory, face to face with Christ, I could do a more real good than by an Act of Parliament against slums or immorality or sweating, or by personal service. The latter is preventive. The former is curative.

But how can the Church do this for the world if its members have not done it for themselves ? Half-cured invalids are not efficient doctors and nicely veneered pagans are not very effective prophets. Men who have become used to dug-outs make poor leaders over the top at dawn. And the matter comes

67

down to us all as a personal message, to get the first thing right for ourselves.

John Wesley went out as a missionary to Georgia, to lift the life of Red Indians. He was an ordained clergyman of the Church of England. The Church of England was, and is, a wonderful organisation; but John Wesley, as a missionary, was a failure. Like many of us he was a veneered pagan, a creature of the dug-out, though he read his Bible and said his prayers. But one night in a little room in Aldersgate Street, London, his heart was strangely warmed. He got the first thing right himself. He wrote in his diary, "I knew that He had taken away *my* sins, even mine, and saved me." Then he climbed on his horse and went through England like a blazing torch lit from the altar-fires of God, and a historian wrote, "The man who saved England in the 18th century was John Wesley." But he was not a man merely who could defend his faith from an intellectual standpoint nor a man who served the Church with zeal. He was a man who had found God. When the men and women in the churches find God their first concern will not be to improve the world. Their passionate desire and purpose will be that the world through them might be *saved*. They will be a group of young people of all ages who have found that experience of Christ which makes the New Testament the most thrilling book in the world, and who seek to change the whole world by passing that experience on.

IV
IN OUR FAMILIARITY
WITH RELIGION?

IN OUR FAMILIARITY
WITH RELIGION?

WHEN Olive Schreiner was a little girl she got hold of a copy of the New Testament and began to read it. Before she got past the early chapters of St. Matthew she rushed into her mother's room and said, " Oh, Mummy, look what I've found ! Isn't it lovely ? Now we can all live like this." The new world that Christ offers was indeed new to her. Therefore it had a grip on her imagination which perhaps we, who have been nurtured in the Christian faith, can never know.

We must be careful here. I owe so much to a good Christian home that I would write no word which could possibly be interpreted as a disparagement of what is perhaps the finest foundation that can ever be laid for any life. At the same time there is a very real danger in a conventional Christian home. As someone has said, "We can be so inoculated by small doses of Christianity that we can't catch the big thing." We can be so familiar with the phrases which describe religious experiences that we think we have had them when we haven't, or rather, we think that what we have experienced is all that there is to experience.

One of the things which hold back progress in modern Church life is the presence of vast numbers of people who not only have had no real experience of God, but who do not believe there is anything to find save what they have found. They are a dead weight which the Church has to carry, and at one point after another they spoil the Church's witness because the so-called outsider judges the value of religion from them. The Church says to the outsider, "Come and join us and find what we've found." The outsider replies, "If what you've found makes you what you are, I don't

74

think I want it." And often he is right, for we all prefer cheerful paganism to a gloomy and spurious Christianity—Charlie Chaplin to the purely professional parson who speaks the name of Christ glibly enough but does not remind us of Him. Thousands of alleged Christians—some of them in the pulpit and hundreds holding office—are hiding from God in the dug-out of familiarity. Take an actual illustration. Here is Alice, the daughter of a Christian home, always regular in her attendance at church, at class, at communion, whose parents are keen church workers. She would tell you that she has always been a Christian. Alice always has by her bedside, *Daily Light*, *In His Steps*, *Being and Doing*, *The Pilot*, and *Thomas à Kempis*. What, in so many cases, is all that has happened? She has become what conditions made her, and that is all. Here is Angela, whose father and mother are gipsies. She is brought up in a gipsy camp. She is taught to lie and steal and drink. What has happened ? She has yielded to her environment, and that is all. Let Alice thank God for her conditions, but she must not claim that her second-hand righteousness is her own volitional possession any more than Angela's second-hand vice is her own free choice. Both have just yielded to environment and are what that environment has made them. Both may be hiding from God ; and if that is so, we must be much more violent with Alice, because a Sunday school class is a better cover from God, a deeper dug-out, a better defence against self-knowledge, than stealing.

One is tempted to develop the differences between them. Alice is in danger of supposing that she is " saved." Angela is free from that danger, and some spiritual impact finds Angela more easily than it finds Alice, who is so cleverly inoculated by small doses of religion against spiritual infection. Therefore the conversion of Angela is satisfying, full of wonder and rapture, whereas for Alice it is much

76

harder to find reality in religion at all. Some Alices marry worldly husbands, and then everybody, except God, is surprised when they drop their Sunday school class, Girls' League, and other religious activities. It is simply that once more they yield to conditions. They are chameleons. They are the same colour as their background. They do not possess any real religion of their own.

We can see what a violent spiritual shock is necessary before Alice can really be converted; and many of us are in exactly her place. We have listened to many sermons, attended many conferences, read many books, got a whole host of splendid ideas; but we have never put one of those ideas into practice, and we know in our hearts that we could hardly look into the eyes of Christ and not be afraid of what He saw there—the shallowness, the hypocrisy and unreality of our life.

Recently the Archbishop of Canterbury

invited some clergy to spend a quiet day
in considering their problems together.
One clergyman wrote back and said,
" Your Grace, in my village we do not
need a quiet day, we need an earthquake."
It is so with many within the Church.
Our very familiarity with the phrases
which describe great experiences block
us from the experiences. Our attendance
at Church services has become dope.
Watch a great congregation singing a
hymn set to a well-known tune and from
their facial expressions you will know
that they are not meaning the tremendous
words they are singing—words often
of utter surrender, words of flame written
by some mystic in an hour of intense
exaltation following weeks and months
of self-discipline. Indeed the hearty swing
with which some of our services " go "
is just as dangerous as it can be. It
produces a spurious substitute for true
religion, a substitute in which there is
no power and reality for the business of
living. Good tunes and hearty services

can become very powerful drugs to put the soul to sleep.

Was it not this very refuge from reality which we have called familiarity with religion which called forth the violent language of Jesus? The Scribes and Pharisees were the most religious people of His day. But they would not hear. They could not believe that there was anything to discover that they had not discovered. The common people heard Him gladly. For them He opened up a new world. It was comparatively easy to win them. But the hardest people in the world to win are those who do not believe there lies anything beyond them which they do not already know, and who hate to be disturbed.

Such people are the Pharisees of to-day. Consciously honest, many of them, as those of old; unconsciously hiding from the God they say they seek, they do exactly what the Pharisees of old did. They pretended Jesus was mistaken or His teaching impracticable, so that they could go on sleeping. They were shocked so that they might look the other way. They persecuted Him, so that they might be spared looking into their own hearts. And Jesus was violent with them with a violence which was the measure of His love and the measure of the depth of their dug-out and the measure of the urgency of their spiritual condition.

Recently someone said that the way of Jesus is largely ignored because people do not understand what He wants them to do. "His world was so different, so less complex than ours. His message was all right for His age, but it cannot be worked out for this age." See the old dodge of pretending He is wrong! I am afraid the answer is that people ignore Him, not because they do not understand Him, but because they do understand Him, and because He calls them to a way of life which would make them greater than they dare to be. And perhaps modern preaching is too safe, not intolerant enough, not hard enough, not strong enough, not austere enough, not disturbing enough, not violent enough to shell men out of those trenches and grooves which so easily and insidiously deepen into dug-outs and graves.

And now, in a sense, the problem is more acute in that those very words of Jesus which smashed men's complacency, and were strange and disturbing enough to break the frozen ice of the familiar, are themselves familiar.

Watch any congregation while the lesson is being read. They look, for the most part, bored and indifferent. *They have heard it all before.* Some of us would give almost anything if by some magic we could bring about such a change in the minds of those who attend our Churches that the words of the Gospels should fall upon their ears and make the impression on their minds and hearts and con- sciences which was made on those who heard the words for the first time. Every teacher and preacher knows the horror of realising that he is saying things that

81

F

are of vital importance to his hearers and yet he cannot find words which get through the armour of familiarity which guards the hearts before him from any disturbing shaft.

It is astonishing, when one comes to read the Gospels with a mind emptied of preconceptions, that our characteristic picture of Jesus should be one which so definitely emphasises the gentle aspects of His nature. These aspects are quite true and we need not unlearn them. We ought, however, to correct our picture of Jesus and of the nature and impact of His message by looking at the other side of His character. He was far from being easy-going or tolerant in the weak sense ; far from possessing that character whose slogan is " peace at any price " ; far from being the kind of person who would pass over our slackness, sins and spiritual anæmia. I should think that to meet Him—unless our souls were already all but dead within us—would either bring us over to His side with a surrender more complete than we have ever known, or else make us look to our defences, entrench ourselves further in, find stronger reasons for not following His way of life, and thicken our cushioned compromises so as not to feel the thrust of His personality.

We may speak of His gentleness and kindness if we will, as long as we remember that the impact of His personality on very many who listened to Him must have been more like dynamite than dew. " I came not to send peace but a sword. For I am come to set a man at variance against his father, and the daughter against her mother, and the daughter in law against her mother in law. And a man's foes shall be they of his own household. He that loveth father or mother more than Me is not worthy of Me ; and he that loveth son or daughter more than Me is not worthy of Me. And he that taketh not his cross and followeth after Me, is not worthy of Me." " I am come to send fire on the earth ;

and what will I, if it be already kindled."
There is a kind of violence about sentences
like these.

Listen to a congregation singing, " But
sweeter far Thy face to see, and in Thy
presence rest," and it would seem as
though His presence was as sweet and
languid as a summer evening in which
one can bask among flowers and gaze
dreamily up at the blue sky and listen to
the hum of the bees. But the Pharisees
did not find it like that. " Ye generation of vipers, how shall ye escape the
damnation of Hell ? " That breaks the
picture. It must have shocked them to
the depths. And if one can get behind
the printed words and see the stern Face
and blazing Eyes, there would not be
much resting in His presence left.

So with those fearful sentences beginning, " Woe unto you hypocrites."
If you had heard Him say to you, " Thou
hypocrite ! " it would be a long time
before you would remember, " Gentle
Jesus, meek and mild." And even to

His own friends He would turn round with the violence that seems as though it would shatter a friendship, " Get thee behind me, Satan "—the measure of His violence being, surely, the measure of His appreciation of the subtlety of the temptation coming to Him from the lips of a friend.

It is He again who uses those violent expressions about cutting off the hand or the foot or plucking out the eye. It is a violent phrase ; but when we have whittled it down as much as we like, it still remains that Jesus believes it were better to give up your job (that is, what the hand finds to do) than to imperil the soul ; to leave the path of life you are treading (that is, where the feet go) than to let some path which we cannot justify in our best moments lead us to spiritual death. It is better in His view to lead what might be called " a one-eyed life " than, in another phrase, " to see life " and find our soul in toils.

We preach His words and people listen

and go home and put on their slippers
and yawn and say, " Quite a good congregation this evening," or some such every-
day remark ; and they go to bed feeling
that they have, by attending Church,
paid a tribute to God. But when Jesus
preached His first sermon the whole
place was in an uproar. They cast Him
out of the synagogue, nearly hounded
Him over the precipice near the village.
There was a violence and a dynamic
about Him that simply knocked men
out of their grooves and made them
challenge Him and challenge themselves.

Such a challenge, such a violence is
essential with those who are familiar
with religion for they are the hardest to
win. And the barrier of familiarity is
one of the hardest to overcome. Of
course Jesus can smash all our barriers ;
but He will not. Even His violence is
the violence of love, which has what
one is almost compelled to call a dreadful
respect for personality. He will not
override our will. He will use argument,

violence of words; He will even induce fear; He will certainly give Himself with that utter self-giving of which the Cross is the eternal symbol in order to save us, but ultimately it is we who must respond. Sometimes we wish He would smash down the door and take possession; but He stands before it with His everlasting word, "Behold I stand at the door and knock." He will besiege but not burgle the soul.

I can only ask you to listen to that language, the violence of which is the measure of His concern and His love. If you think religion is a side-issue to which you can be indifferent and careless and procrastinating, I ask you to listen to His language again and then look at His Cross, and you will realise His conception of the importance of your personal relationship with God. The man who is passionate and intense about something that doesn't matter vitally is the crank, the faddist, the fanatic. Do you think He is one of these? I think

not. Does He care so much about
something that doesn't matter either way ?
It cannot be. His eyes are on you,
burning you, piercing you, holding you.
Your heart wavers, is wistful, is longing,
your only hope of peace of mind, of being
what you yourself in your best moments
want to be, and of being what He died
to make you, is to come to Him and
utterly to surrender yourself to Him.
He will tell you what to do. He will
begin with you where you are. He will
never let you go.

V
IN MISUSING RELIGION
TO EVADE REALITY?

IN MISUSING RELIGION
TO EVADE REALITY?

WE who are said to be seeking for God are often hiding from Him in that we are misusing religion to evade reality.

There has arisen a school of psychologists who decry religion because, they say, it is a flight from reality and an evasion of the challenge of life. " Here is a man," they say, " who does not like the thought that death is the end, so he makes up a belief in immortality. He does not like to think of the injustice of life, so he pretends all will be put right hereafter. As he grows up he feels the need of a father-substitute. In the universe as science reveals it he feels lonely and afraid. So he makes up a picture of a ' Heavenly Father.' He would fain talk to this Person so he prays to Him, forgetting that any value prayer has can be explained by the phenomenon of auto-suggestion."

This position is partly met if we remember that the symbol of Christianity is not a feather bed into which a man can creep snugly to evade the shocks of this hard world. It is a Cross. It is a Cross offered to men by Jesus as well as endured by Him. And has any idea sent so many men out to lonely self-sacrifice, heroic adventure, and the death of the martyr as the religion we call Christianity?

Yet such critics as I have indicated are not wholly beside the mark. There *is* a kind of spurious religion to which many people do fly in order to escape the challenges of life. It is not Christianity. It is a substitute for it. It is one of its most deadly enemies. For from the first inception by Christ of the principles of Christianity we may note that one of its most powerful enemies has always been what is misnamed religion. Christ was crucified by religious people who do it again now even while they bow before His cross. And many who consider themselves religious have got this spurious substitute, a smug, complacent, conventional sham in which they hide, from which they are hard to drive out, and in the enjoyment of which they hate to be disturbed. It is this insincere, unreal, hypocritical, counterfeit thing made of easy compromise that makes " religious " people the best hated in the world by the jolly pagan. Let them realise that it is not religion but a bastard substitute, not a tonic but a drug, an anæsthetic, a species of dope, a subtle means of hiding from God, used by many who are supposed to have found Him.

I do not mean, of course, that religion is never to be an escape from life. There is a sense in which religion ought to be, and is, a shelter for the soul from the hard knocks of life. The psalmists revelled in that conception. They spoke of God as a shield, a strong tower, a fortress. They spoke of the secret place of the most High, of the shadow of the Almighty, and of being covered with His pinions and taking refuge under His wings. And though we do not lay as much stress as did the Jews on this aspect of religion yet we often call a church a sanctuary, in which word is a whole wealth of meaning; and the rougher the life we have to live the more do we understand the meanings associated with that word. I can remember during army days with what relief, and even with a sense of escape, some of us revelled in the services that were held in a chapel composed of two tents strung together. The place became holy ground. You could get away from the crude roughness of active service and sing the old hymns and think about other things until a hush fell upon the spirit and God became real again. Often now I find myself almost envying people who have no responsibility for a Church service, who can slip within hallowed walls made sacred by many years' devotion, and can forget their cares and worries and find a real sense of escape for an hour at least, and can then find when they go back to shoulder the burden again, that, although the burden is not lighter, they have acquired a greater strength to carry it.

If we begin to analyse the origin of this sense of escape, this shelter of the soul, we should find it not so much in the building with all its mental associations, though these are a help. We should find it mainly, I think, in the idea of God which we most need and which in our distress is the particular medicine which we can appropriate to ourselves.

Supposing there enters a church a man who has slipped into some sin and who is genuinely sorry and distressed. I like to think that he will find healing, whatever the hymns and lessons and sermon may be about. He will find that healing partly in the presence of God and partly because, as his mind dwells on God, he will mentally absorb that particular idea about God which meets his own special

95

need. In this case he would take the idea that God forgives. He shelters his soul, that is, in the forgiving love of God. He realises that God is the kind of person who, when we are penitent, puts our sins behind His back, blots them out, remembers them no more for ever, and sets us free, with the relationship between ourselves and God absolutely restored as if no sin had ever broken it. It is an amazing and liberating thought, and as it permeates a man's mind it sends him out with new courage, new hope, new purpose to face again the shining way. This is one of the real and legitimate ways in which religion supplies what we may call a shelter for the soul.

But there is a very real danger, which, as I said above, the psychologists have clearly seen, that religion may become a species of dope. We must not blind ourselves to the fact that religion is very attractive from the mere point of selfishness. It offers an inward peace, splendid hopes, and promises which reach even unto a future life. It is good to realise that there is another side to all the comfort of religion ; a side which is a challenge. We sing regularly a very beautiful hymn, " Hark, hark my Soul." There is something wonderfully appealing and soothing in some of the words :

Far, far away, like bells at evening pealing,
  The voice of Jesus sounds o'er land and sea,
And laden souls, by thousands meekly stealing,
  Kind Shepherd, turn their weary steps to Thee.

And I don't mean to suggest for a moment that there is not in religion a shelter for these meek souls. But there is another side to it all. When the voice of Jesus sounded first it wasn't "far, far away," but uncomfortably near and challenging. It wasn't so much like a bell at evening. It was like a trumpet at dawn. It did not call to rest and peace and quietness, but to adventure and sacrifice and death. That is what I mean by an illicit shelter of the soul. To expect to find comfort and peace and rest without

97

G

carrying out the obligations involved is to seek an illicit shelter of the soul, and so far from finding God it is to evade the real God. As Dr. Fosdick says, " Every Christian truth, gracious and comfortable, has a corresponding obligation, searching and sacrificial."

Look for a moment at another shelter, God's love for the individual. What a shelter for the lonely soul! " None is so small or insignificant," says this lovely message, " but God thinks about him and knows all his needs. God's love goes down below the individual to the sparrow that falls to the ground." I could expend much space developing that glorious theme. Yet when it was preached it was not preached so much to comfort the lonely in the audience as to challenge that audience to impersonate in themselves God's love for other individuals, and to claim them in a campaign for the unfortunate. Jesus is not only uttering words of consolation to us, but saying in other words that those who think human

98

personality is as sacred as those words suggest must stand to others as men who try to represent God and to care for the lonely and oppressed wherever they find them. To fly to one side of the teaching without the other is an illicit shelter of the soul which is dope and self-deception rather than religion. It is not finding God, but misusing religion to evade Him.

And although it may be suggested that it is a harmless kind of dope, it is not so harmless as we may think, because it tends to make all religion unworthy. It will cut out from religion the spirit of service, and this will poison religion in the soul, just as a lake which receives the mountain stream and does not give it out again to the valley below will become not a lake but a morass of stagnation and poison. Men who simply seek a kind of illicit shelter for their soul in religion will find religion as an isolated kind of experience which has little power to help them, and it will be to them like a memory of some song they heard years ago, vague and distant and unrelated to life. Jesus doesn't say, "If you follow Me life will be crowned with a wreath of roses." He indicates quite clearly that most probably it will be crowned with thorns. Religion is not dope nor insurance nor escape. It is conquest, because man is placed in touch with such amazing resources that whatever happens nothing can conquer his spirit. The things that happen to others will not pass us by. We shall not be saved from them, but saved in them. We shall not escape them, but we shall escape fear of them. We shall be shown how to triumph over them. And if we could only receive it, what happens to us doesn't matter. What matters is our reaction to what happens to us. The man who has found God has not insured himself against calamity. But he has found One who will show him how to turn calamity into triumph. He will not escape the thorns of life. But he will wear them as a crown.

VI
IN A REFUSAL OF RIGHT RELATIONS WITH MEN?

IN A REFUSAL OF RIGHT RELATIONS WITH MEN?

THE New Testament makes it very clear that a search for God on the part of an individual who will not put his relationships with men right is a hopeless proceeding. For this reason alone, many, in their search for God, fail. One friend of mine for two years sought for the kind of experience of God which the New Testament offers in such glowing colours and about which he had heard others speak. Then it came home to him that he wanted a private experience of God which would bring him comfort, peace and strength, but he was unwilling to put away a grievance and resentment which he bore another. He sought out that other, talked things over, asked forgiveness for the malice in his heart and since then he has become one of the most radiant Christian men I know.

" If therefore thou art offering thy gift at the altar and there rememberest that thy brother hath ought against thee, leave there thy gift before the altar; first be reconciled to thy brother and then come and offer thy gift."

We have seen already the need for repentance. For, indeed, we need forgiveness. But it is well to point out that the condition Jesus mentions which is essential to forgiveness is not repentance, but our forgiveness of others. " It is often said that our Lord's doctrine is that of free forgiveness on the sole condition of repentance; but if by forgiveness is meant the readiness and desire to restore the old relations of love and intimacy then there are no conditions at all. God always and unceasingly desires to maintain those relations and to restore these as soon as ever we break them. But there is a condition that we must fulfil if we are to make our own the forgiveness He always and freely offers. And it is noticeable that repentance is not, in fact, mentioned in this action. The one thing that is mentioned, and that with a most solemn reiteration, is our forgiveness of those who have injured us or are in our debt. The prayer for forgiveness is the only petition in the Lord's Prayer to which any condition is is attached ; and it is this condition. The lesson is driven home by the Parable of the Unforgiving Servant " (Matt. xviii, 23-35).[1] There is no such thing as a private reconciliation with God as long as relationships with men are not as right as we can make them. A religion which neglects this tremendous truth is that most subtle and deadly thing, a perversion of religion, a self-deception, a comfortable way of escaping reality.

God, we have made clear, is seeking us, but we cannot be found and restored to the relationship with His other children if there is a single one of them whom we refuse to forgive. A boy who will not

[1] Archbishop Temple, *Christ's Revelation of God*, p. 37 (S.C.M.).

be friends with his brothers cannot privately be received by his father. A boy who sought his father with the reservation that he mustn't be asked to be friendly with all his brothers would show how woefully wrong was his conception of family life. Yet that is what men and women within the Church are constantly doing. We see them standing up and singing hymns, even kneeling at the Communion Table, and yet we know they regard one person as a "rank outsider" and another as "hopelessly impossible"; that they say of one, "I've washed my hands of him," and of another, "I've no use for him," and of a third (condescendingly), "I forgive him, but I hope I shan't meet him again." No such soul will ever find God in the New Testament sense until that proud conceit is broken down. The God such folk think they have found is a caricature such as Mr. Bernard Shaw delights to portray.[1] Such a God is not the Father of Jesus.

[1] cf. *The Black Girl in her Search for God.*

No real contact could be maintained with Jesus by a soul which harboured resentment or left wrong without whatever restitution was possible being made. We note this in the case of Zaccheus. Christ did not tell Zaccheus to make restitution. Zaccheus knew that his relationship with Jesus could not be right, knew that a rich experience was being held back, until wrong things were put right. " If I have wronged any man I will restore him fourfold."

Often it is not so easy for us as for Zaccheus. To pay back money is not difficult if we possess it. Often it is not easy to see what needs to be done to put our relationship right. A confession of sin to the wronged person is not always the right thing to do. It may give the sinner relief by placing the burden he carries in his conscience as an added burden on the shoulders of the one already wronged. This was so, for example, in the case of a man who drugged and then sexually assaulted his victim.

But for most of us it is not so hard to see what we *ought* to do. What is hard is the blow to our pride involved in doing what we see to be right.

Not every attempt to put right a relationship with men is met with tears of joy and the outstretched hand. Sometimes such an attempt is met with silence or contempt or with the shrugged shoulder or with that secret malice which rejoices that the enemy has "climbed down." In spite of this let us get our relationships as right as we can, for only so can we find God. If we have robbed another of his good name let us tell him so, ask his forgiveness and try to repair the damage we have done. If we have harboured jealous thoughts, or bitter, unkind criticisms of another, let us tell him so and be more loving, tolerant and charitable. If we have parted from another in anger let us seek him out or write him at once and seek to put matters right. If we are seeking God let us first spend some time in thinking out our relationships with men, making arrangements for certain interviews, posting half a dozen letters. And if the person wronged be dead or removed beyond our ken, or if confession would make the situation more intolerable than ever for the wronged person, let us solemnly acknowledge that wrong before God and dedicate ourselves to a more devoted service of sympathy to the kind of victim we have wronged, and of preventive and alert service to the kind of sinner we have been, acknowledging to the latter, if need be, our own fall, that he may be saved from becoming what we already have become.

Dr. Frank Buchman tells us that his conversion involved the writing of six letters to men whom he felt he had wronged. He did not get six replies but he did get a tremendous sense of personal release. He found God in a way he had never found Him before. And the story of the Oxford Group Movement abounds in illustrations of our theme. Here is a man at the head of a printing plant in the East. He seeks a full experience of God. One morning he says something like this, " You men have worked because you feared me. That is all wrong. From now on Christ is the head of this business." Having apologised to an Indian with whom he had lost his temper, he put all the three hundred employees on a living wage, and because relationships were right he himself entered into a transforming experience of the power and love of God. A doctor I know put right a relationship with the examiners who formed the authority which gave him his degree, though he risked losing it altogether. One man offered a former employer £250 as payment for a thousand hours stolen from him when he should have been working. Mr. A. J. Russell's book, *For Sinners Only*, is crammed with stories of men and women who have found God, and their cases strongly support our theme.

It is no good saying, " Well, I admit that my relationship *with Christ* is wrong but I shall get over it. Time will heal the trouble." What a dreary lie it is that time heals everything ! Does time heal a suppurating appendix or a repressed complex or a sense of guilt ? All three require surgical help. The first applied to the body, the second to the mind, the third to the soul. And the third kind of surgery is the painful setting right as far as possible of our relationships with men. Neglect that surgery and the body may die, the mind be disabled, the spirit crippled by a depression from which a man cannot be aroused by any other treatment. This is not a warning carelessly written down. Indeed what warning could be more stern than this ? " When ye pray say . . . ' Forgive us our trespasses as we forgive them that trespass against us.' *For if ye forgive not men their trespasses neither will your Heavenly Father forgive you your trespasses.*"[1]

[1] Matt. vi, 15.

But I want to pass to another sense in which we miss God because we want Him for ourselves and would exclude our relations with others from our quest. It must be realised that we cannot live by ourselves in the little house of life, and shut and bar the doors, and put " No hawkers; no circulars " on the gate, and proceed to find God. Do we really love our brother? Or do we shrink from contact with him? True, he is not always lovable. He is vain, selfish, cruel, unsympathetic, critical and so on. Even so we cannot be religious and selfish. The two words imply opposites. The life that shuts itself off from its fellows will not find God.

We recall the phrase in the Benedictus,

That we should be saved from our enemies
And from the hand of all that hate us.

But is it a good thing that we should be delivered from the hands of all that hate us? Might it not be a very good thing for us to hear what they have to say ? Might not they be the servants of God doing His work ? With Browning we may ask, " Hush, I pray you. What if that friend—or even apparent enemy—happens to be God ? "

We know how some foolish mothers receive their child after he has had his face smacked, say, by another boy : " There ! there ! did that horrid boy tease you and hit you, then ? " Mark Sabre in *If Winter Comes* is always flying out of the room saying that his wife doesn't understand him. Do we not seek God in much the same way, wearing the mood of injured innocence, fleeing from men who misunderstand us, revile us, yes, and hate us, and expect God to pat us on the head, and say, " There ! there ! they are nasty horrid people to misunderstand you." Probably the nasty horrid people are also going to God complaining about you. That is to say we seek in God a refuge and an escape from men who, if we listened to them and heeded their criticisms, might add steel and grit

113

H

to our character. Isn't that what Jesus means by loving your enemies; not fleeing from them but listening to them patiently without losing your temper, hearing them out, doing the fair thing by them? And do we, by our attempt to escape, deprive God of His intention to find us more fully through them? It is because this has been so, that religion has earned its name of being soft; of being what some psychologists call an infantile attitude to life, for we try to make it an escape from life. Browning has a word for us here:

Then, welcome each rebuff
That turns earth's smoothness rough,
　　Each sting that bids nor sit nor stand but go!
Be our joys three-parts pain!
Strive, and hold cheap the strain;
　Learn, nor account the pang; dare, never grudge
　　　the throe.
He fixed thee mid this dance
Of plastic circumstance,
　　This Present, *thou, forsooth, wouldst fain arrest:*
Machinery just meant
To give thy soul its bent,
　　Try thee, and turn thee forth, sufficiently im-
　　　pressed.

Let me tell you a true story which moved me very much. A friend of mine is a minister working among miners. During a strike he tried a most interesting and successful experiment. He organised on his church premises a toy factory. The miners made toys and sold them, and in this way, in many miners' homes, they kept the wolf from the door. My friend told me how the men revelled in it. It gave them food for their minds, and brought food to their bodies at a time when, in some other places, miners were standing at street corners or sitting in public houses. My friend himself worked with them. He had the exquisite joy which I, at any rate, have never had, of having made something with his hands. He says the men worked early and late, putting in far more hours than any mine owners ever asked for. At the same time —though my friend never said so—I imagine the miners sometimes got on his nerves. On one occasion he went for a long walk in order to be alone. He wanted to be alone, and pray, and be quiet. He simply could not get away from the sound of footsteps. If he stopped on the road he heard footsteps coming. He dawdled till they overtook him and then waited, but there always were some others. He left the road and went into a wood. He really thought he was getting alone and quiet. He began to pray. Then tramp, tramp, tramp . . . . He could still hear men walking on the road below him. At one point he took to his heels and ran, and stopped, panting, waiting . . . . his breath came in sobs . . . . Then on a road he never knew existed he heard the same noise of footsteps, tramp, tramp, tramp . . . . He felt like a man pursued, frantic, desperate . . . . He did so want to get away from men, he did so want the refuge of God . . . . Yet always the sound of following feet . . . . tramp, tramp, tramp. Then a voice came to him from God which might have expressed its message in the words of Francis Thompson :

Still with unhurrying chase,
And unperturbed pace,
  Deliberate speed, majestic instancy,
Came on the following Feet,
And a Voice above their beat,
  Naught shelters thee, who wilt not shelter
    Me.

The feet were the feet of God. The feet all around him were telling him that the life that excludes men cannot find God.

Do not misunderstand. There are times when we must shut men out physically. Every Christian must be a believer in the shut door, the secret place. We must make times when we push away the tumultuous demands of things and men and get alone with God. But though we must shut them out of our rooms we mustn't shut them out of our prayers or out of our hearts. We must shut people out physically as Jesus did ; but we must not shut them out spiritually. Jesus never did. Jesus says " Go into the inner room and shut the door and pray in secret." But He says, " pray for those who despitefully use you." Shut them

117

out of your room, but not out of your heart.

I think the great part of the truth of this part of my message can be expressed in a parable of a little boy whose father was the medical officer in charge of a big institution for the blind. One evening when it was getting dark one of the blind patients came to the door of the medical officer's house. As it happened the little boy was just going upstairs to bed. He had one glimpse of the sightless eyes of the man at the door and then he rushed off screaming and terrified. His father picked the laddie up and hushed his baby terror, taking him right away to his own study in another part of the building; and then when terror and fear had been banished, the father took his laddie with him and they went and spoke to the blind man. The father explained that all his own life's interest lay in helping those people. The boy grew up to love them and ultimately to serve them. Notice! If the father had only taken the boy away to his study to comfort him, the experience would have been robbed of more than half its potential value. The boy would have had a repressed fear of blindness which might have wrought in him positive harm. One might be certain he would not have grown up to love the blind, as he did first for his father's sake and then for their sake as well.

It is not different for us. Surely we may turn to God as a refuge, a hiding place, a covert, but then we must turn back to men, loving them in spite of their criticisms, their meannesses, their disloyalties, and our experience of men will bring us nearer to the real God and we shall learn how best He may be served. There is a time when the fretted soul may be in his lover's arms. But, except in novels, *men* do not stay long in their lover's arms. They go back to duty. And because they have been in their lover's arms, if the lover is worth the name, they are stronger, braver, better men.

It seems to me that Charles Wesley is teaching us this lesson in one of his most popular hymns.

> Jesu, Lover of my soul,
>   Let me to Thy bosom fly.
>
> Other refuge have I none,
>   Hangs my helpless soul on Thee,
> Leave, ah leave me not alone,
>   Still support and comfort me.
> All my trust on Thee is stayed,
>   All my help from Thee I bring,
> Cover my defenceless head
>   With the shadow of Thy wing.

How the mind rests in that sure and great refuge! But listen. A man does not stay long in the Lover's arms. The soul is beginning to be satisfied.

Thou, O Christ, art all I want.—This is a much stronger note than

> Hide me, O my Saviour hide.

This is the beginning of satisfaction. Then what happens? The mind begins to go out to others.

> Raise the fallen, cheer the faint,
> Heal the sick, and *lead the blind*.

And there is the implication that that must be done through man's co-operation.

The wonderful story of the Transfiguration reveals this principle in the Master's life. The Master has sought refuge, escape, sanctuary. He wanted, I think, escape from men as well as from things. On the lonely mountain peak, alone with the three who understood, He is finding peace, poise, quietness, harmony. We cannot follow Him very far into this experience. The Son is back in the bosom of the Father. This kind of communion is higher than we have ever known. The fashion of His countenance is altered. His very raiment is white and glistening. All this is beyond us as it was beyond those who were with Him. We kneel with them in utter awe. We feel with them as men who have no right to be there, however good it is to be allowed to share the experience. Peter is quite out of his depth. He is the practical man and the impulsive man. He doesn't quite like it. It seems uncanny. It is an experience too vast, too deep, too high for him. He wants to make something ; to do something with his hands. He submits a proposal. " Let us make three shelters— one for Thee, and one for Moses and one for Elijah," and Mark, his biographer, probably at Peter's own instance, adds in the record, " For he wist not what to say, for they were sore afraid." A cloud, shot through and through with the sunlight, kisses the mountain peak, and it seems a symbol to Peter of the presence of the very God. God is talking to His own Son. Yes, and God, through that very experience, is talking to them, saying, " This is my beloved Son, hear ye Him ! " Far below seethes the multitude. But here all is quiet. Then do you see what follows ? " And when they were come to the multitude there came a man kneeling to Him and saying, ' Lord have mercy on my son for he is an epileptic ' . . . ." And Jesus healed the boy. He was cured from that hour.

Back from refuge to reality. Not escaping from life, but finding, in the place of refuge, power for life and meaning in life.

We must do that. We must not go to church Sunday after Sunday and just feel how beautiful it all is. We must not get half-hypnotised by the lights and music and devotional atmosphere. We shall not find God in any enduring way unless we link Sunday night with Monday morning; and unless Monday morning is different because of Sunday night we may ask whether we really get to God on Sunday night or only deceive ourselves. Because of this many ardent churchgoers have never found God at all. We shall not get further with our problem than Jesus did in Gethsemane. Into those woods He went for refuge, for escape, for sanctuary—refuge from men as well as from things. He gets away, there, even from His dearest. He went forward a little, and fell on the ground, and there prayed. He wanted the Father's arms about Him, those everlasting arms.

But a man never stays long in the arms of his Lover . . . "Arise, let us be going; he that betrayeth Me is at hand." Into the woods He went, anguished, doubting, troubled. Out of the woods He came, from refuge to reality, calm, confident, unafraid. "This is the way the Master went. Should not the servant tread it still?" You are seeking God, you say? What is your relation to men?

VII
BEHIND OTHER CLOSED DOORS ?

BEHIND OTHER CLOSED DOORS?

LET us, in the final chapter of this section, group together some other things that may be between us and the great discovery of God. The picture in my mind is that of a back-water shut from the great flowing river by a sluice-gate that is closed. If I open the sluice-gate then the pure rushing waters of the great river will come surging in, cleansing, refreshing and bringing new life through every part of the back-water. If I keep the gate shut my back-water, however near the river, will be a stagnant unbeautiful place.

The energies of God are very near us. If we do not know the power, serenity, joy and love which He offers by His indwelling, it must be that somewhere a sluice-gate is closed against Him. Perhaps if we are honest we *know* what that gate is. A secret sin we will not give up, a faulty relationship we will not put right.

But room must be made for that trick of the human mind which the psychologists call "rationalisation"—the giving of a false reason for conduct because the real reason is distasteful, like the old lady climbing the mountain who said, "I think we will rest here. This is the best place to see the view." In reality, of course, she was "puffed."

Room must also be made for the fact that such rationalisation can sink into the mind by repetition until it becomes truly unconscious. We do not consciously realise that the reason we give is not the real reason of our conduct. We talk of "righteous indignation" when the real label is "bad temper." We speak of determination when "pig-headedness" would be nearer the mark. We say we had to "speak out" when really we are quarrelsome; and so on. To keep our figure, the sluice-gate can get so covered with slime and weed that we do not perceive that there *is* a door which is shut against God.

In such a case we must stop " looking for God " and look for the door that keeps Him out. We must pray for the Holy Spirit to reveal this deep thing to us. We must ask our real friends to tell us plainly the things that spoil our life.

Look at some of them briefly.

1. We can be quite sure that very often it is a disguised selfishness. Self is too much in the picture. Even in our prayers we are praying largely for ourselves. We want God for what we can get out of Him. When we are doing something for others it becomes a subtle form of self-flattery and we pat ourselves on the back for doing it. When we engage in any kind of service we are watching ourselves with one eye. " Am I going to get anything out of this ? " or " Am I going to appear in this to advantage ? " In other words the whole life revolves round the self, the life is egocentric

129

I

instead of theocentric. And we shall only find God when He shows us how to put ourselves right out of the picture, only asking for His glory—even willing to look fools and to be unpopular and to be lonely if His purposes can be achieved and His glory enhanced.

2. Another thing that so often gets in our way is a love of sin going hand in hand with a love of righteousness. We pray to be delivered from sins without remembering that sin only grows in the heart that gives it room. What so often happens is that, in certain moods of the soul, we want God and within twenty-four hours we want sin even more. We must ask Him to show us the nature of sin, how it blinds us, and binds us, and wounds Him, so that we come to hate it with our whole being instead of with half our mind. The shut door for many lives is a secret love of some form of sin which is being rationalised by the conscience.

3. Another door that we shut against

God is the fear of what people will say and think. One finds this again and again in business life. A youngster goes from school to an office with high ideals and with earnest desires to live a Christian life, but it is very hard to be good by yourself. The youngster, whether boy or girl, does not want to be thought pious or goody-goody, so when the dirty story goes round, rather shame-facedly, he laughs. He puts a shilling on a horse. With the rest he gradually begins to rationalise his conduct by phrases like " Everybody does it," and " Being a sport," and so on. We must ask Him to make us brave anything, not to be afraid of what people will say or think, once we are sure what is the right thing to do.

4. Another door that we shut against Him is just a suspicion that, after all, the worldling is having a better time than we are. When a man is in process of being found by God he is really standing between two worlds. The world of

Satan and the world of God. He is not bad enough to be completely happy in the world of Satan. He is not good enough to be completely happy in the world of God. When he sees the lovable happy pagan enjoying himself to the full he almost feels affronted. "How dare you be so happy living a life of worldliness when I who am trying to be a Christian am not a bit happy?" The Christian, indeed, has got his bad name for being a wet blanket and for being censorious of worldliness because he is not Christian enough to be quite in God's world, and his criticism of worldliness is inverted envy, which, by the way, is the basis of so much criticism. When a man has entirely surrendered and is completely in God's world his attitude to the worldling is not criticism, but a great longing, mixed with pity, to bring all into the marvellous experience which he has found. Are we shutting a door against God by still desiring the pleasures of worldliness?

5. A fifth door that we shut against God is that of the discipline of keeping in God's world. And here we have the reason why so many who once found God have now nothing that is really vital in their lives. The churches are full of people who, thirty or forty years ago, had a living vital experience of God. In the old phrase they were " converted," in the new phrase they made their " surrender." But, to borrow an illustration from Dr. Jowett, they are like astronomers photographing a star who made no allowance for the revolution of the earth. When an astronomer photographs a star he has to turn his telescope on the star till the light from it falls through the lens on to the photographic plate below. But when this has been done he must remember that though the star is a fixed star the earth is continually revolving and will spoil his adjustment. And it requires a great deal of care to readjust continually if the photograph is to be a picture of the star. There are those

who turned their lives to Christ and had a real experience, but now their experience never sets anybody else on fire because they themselves are not on fire with it. Their Christian experience is the memory of something beautiful that happened twenty or thirty years ago. Every day there must be the readjustment to allow for the pull of the earth and earthly things if our hearts are to become a picture of the star.

Now when once we have found the thing that stands in our way we have more than half-answered our question, " How can I find God ? " There must be the surrender of that which is keeping us from being found of Him, a real surrender involving, if necessary, confession to some suitable friend of the thing that was keeping us back from the great experience.

I shall never forget when my second boy, then a baby of five weeks old, was lying dangerously ill. The general practitioner was very much concerned and worried.

I can see her now turning from the child to me and saying, " He is frightfully ill. I can tell you that much, but I cannot find out what is the matter with him. We must have a specialist."   One of the nightmares of my life was the search for that specialist that night, but, at last, towards midnight, he came. I can see him bending over the body of the child, the fingers of his hand outstretched as though they were eyes that could see through the skin. Then he put his finger on the child's body and said to the doctor, " There is gas there, and there should not be."   The child was wrapped in a blanket, put in his car, taken to a nursing home, operated on, and in a few days had entered into a new kingdom of health.

It may be that you yourself can put your finger on that thing which has never been surrendered, on that point on which you are saying " No " to God. If so, do not talk about looking for God until you have got that right. If not, you must ask this great Surgeon of the Soul to put His finger on the spot and to show you what it is in your life that is holding you back from this tremendous experience which makes Christianity a gospel and the most powerful transforming influence in the world. Do give up playing about with religion and yielding a tepid acquiescence to the Wearer of the Crown of Thorns.

Look finally at this picture. Here is a crowd of people at Capernaum listening to Jesus. On the outskirts of that crowd is a man past middle age whose face we can tenderly read. You notice the lines under his eyes. You notice that he drops his eyes if anybody looks keenly at him. You notice the corners of his mouth turn down and there are heavy lines there, too. You notice the stooping figure and the shuffling gait as he walks homeward when the crowd breaks up. You catch the glint of tears in his eyes. This man is despised by everybody, and that has gone on so long that now he despises himself. The name of his profession is a term of abuse. He is a tax-gatherer. He has stooped to the depths at which a man takes money from his own country-men and hands it over to the hated invader, Rome. This man's name is Matthew. But, when he listened to Jesus, something that was still splendid and not quite dead fluttered within his breast, and as he is going home he is saying to himself: "Yes, it was very beautiful and I should love to be like that, but I am too old. The tracks of habit are too deep and how should I get my living, and what would people say?" He has caught a glimpse of the world that Christ offers, but rather sadly he is shutting the gates, not passing through them. And heavily he turns back to his books, slipping back into the groove that was becoming a grave, the grave of a soul. "But as Jesus passed by He saw Matthew sitting at the receipt of custom." A shadow fell across Mat-thew's ledger on to the page on which but recently the tears of a man growing

old had made the ink run. Matthew
looked up into the eyes that are the homes
of all men's dreams and looking into the
face of Jesus he realised, in a flash, two
things : that Jesus believed in him and
that Jesus knew what was keeping him
back. Knowing his worst, Jesus believed
in his best. The finger of the Great
Physician is on the spot. The eyes of
Jesus are saying, " That is what is stopping
you." And then a voice that drives out
all his fear, fears of the past, fears of the
future, fears of the present. They all
fall away. A voice that breathes incredible strength, a voice that takes
responsibility for all consequences says
to him, " Follow Me." And Matthew
went through the gates into the new
world that Christ offered, the world of
power and joy and peace and love. It
contained martyrdom, but it contained
Jesus, so nothing mattered. That very
day Matthew was with Jesus in paradise,
the world in which God, not self, is the
centre. In the same way, on this day, He

calls you. What are you going to do ? If you make the fullest response you can, He will lead you into an experience greater than anything you have ever known. You will find God.

PART II
HOW MAY WE
FIND HIM ?

I
WHAT DOES FINDING GOD MEAN?

WHAT DOES FINDING
GOD MEAN?

HAVING agreed that our real quest is to be found of God and having, as honestly as we can, searched our own hearts for conscious and semi-conscious barriers which we ourselves have set up, we have yet to ask what " finding God " —to retain the popular expression— really means. I shall not attempt yet to deal with ways in which we may attempt to find Him, nor yet with those effects in life which may result from having found Him. I am trying first of all to set down what we mean when we talk about finding God in the full Christian sense and my definition is this :—" Finding God means entering into a personal, conscious communion, spirit with spirit, with One recognised to be a fitting object of worship and love, in whom we find forgiveness of sin, whose will we desire to do, and in

whom all our highest values are conserved." In its highest form, such as we
see in the life of Jesus, "finding God,"
means that life becomes theocentric. God
is at the very heart of it, and nothing is
done or undertaken or considered apart
from Him, so that His meanings are
flashed from signals we never saw before,
or, seeing, never understood. Joy
became lifted on to a higher plane because
of our relationship with Him. Sorrow
has a different meaning because He is
sharing it with us. Calamity is not
willed for us by Him, but it contains a
challenge from Him and is our opportunity, both of deepening our relationship
with Him, and in His name winning new
power for ourselves. The ordinary
common tasks of life are shot through
and through with His radiance and stand
in a different relationship to life, as beads
scattered on the floor stand in a different
relationship to one another when a single
thread of purpose makes them one. As
someone described it in my Friday Fellow-

ship : " Finding God is having with you a great Comrade who redeems every part of life, keeps you from some dangers because you dare not contemplate the thought of His being in certain places where danger lurks, and makes you able to face circumstances which, without His presence, would be meaningless and dull ! " It therefore emerges that the Christian sense in which the phrase " finding God " is used is unique.

We must, of course, recognise the fact that God is found in other senses far differently and far more easily. Longfellow points out :

> That in even savage bosoms,
> There are longings, yearnings, strivings,
> For the good they comprehend not,
> That the feeble hands and helpless,
> Groping blindly in the darkness,
> Touch God's right hand in the darkness,
> And are lifted up and strengthened.

The savage recognises quite clearly that there is something somewhere which must be worshipped ; but this is not a

personal consciousness of, let alone communion with, One recognised to be a
fitting object of worship and love. He
is commonly not loved by the savage, but
feared, nor are the highest human values
conserved in Him. For God, to the
savage, is often contemplated as doing
things which we should despise, and
which even the savage would despise,
in a man.

A little further up the scale men talk
of " finding God " in nature, in art, in
music. Let us say at once that any man
who has had an experience of beauty,
truth or goodness, recognising them to
be such, has had *an* experience of God.
This fact alone should come with comfort to many and put an end to that
awful loneliness of soul when a man
feels that he is, as it were, on a vast sea
looking for an elusive God. That is
not true of any man. We have all had *an*
experience of God, even though we may
not have had the full Christian experience
of finding him. And we are not in the

position of those who have discovered nothing : aimless wanderers exploring an ocean for some continent, daily scanning the horizon but finding no land to greet our aching eyes. Many would cry with the *Ancient Mariner* :

> . . . This soul hath been
> Alone on a wide, wide sea :
> So lonely 'twas, that God Himself
> Scarce seeméd there to be.

No, we are on the continent. It is not a matter of discovering it. It is a matter of exploring it further, penetrating further in, till it yields its resources and discloses its loveliness. Nature, art, music, literature, law and order, truth and goodness, love and friendship, wherever they are met by the complete human response provide *an* experience of God. A man may hate religion, dislike parsons, be confused by creeds and think church ritual is " tosh," but it is a mark of the divinity of man that he has a faculty to recognise the good, the beautiful, and

149

the true, and there can hardly be a person living who has never touched reality at any of those points. What I want to stress is that when he does touch reality at any of those points it is *an* experience of God.

It will depend on his training and experience, even on his temperament, as to which is his most familiar point of contact with reality, but I do want to emphasise that, whichever it is, it is an experience of God.

Let us look at some illustrations. Here is a man who cannot subscribe to any creeds, who never goes to church, and, indeed, who openly scorns the practice of religion. But let us suppose he is an able mathematician. One day he finds himself wondering at the reliability of mathematical processes, at the universe of law and order which the science of higher mathematics reveals. Must we not say that that moment of wondering is *an* experience of God? Take the astronomer studying the stars. His views on all kinds of theological questions may be chaotic and he may suppose that God plays no part in his life, but he would be a queer astronomer, who, at some moment or other, did not find himself moved—or, let us say, merely impressed, not necessarily emotionally, but intellectually—by astronomy's conception of the movements of the planets. I suggest that that impression is *an* experience of God. Both the mathematician and the astronomer have touched God at the point of truth.

Take any thoughtless young devil-may-care confronted with a glorious landscape ; take the joy of being alive on a June morning when your health is good and nature is opening her loveliness before you ; take some of those young artists of Chelsea studios, who generally, I believe, pose as being irreligious. How God must smile, since their whole appreciation of beauty is *an* experience of Him ! Such an experience is probably as real an experience of God as that of a person emotionally moved by hysterically singing hymns at a revival meeting. The latter would call the artist irreligious. But if the will is untouched in both cases, the hymn singer has no more authentic experience of God than the artist.

Turn to the ultimate of goodness. No one can possibly read the story of Father Damien among the lepers, or even read a newspaper story like that of Captain Oates going out into the snow, without a momentary response, which is the response of any human personality to goodness. That response is *an* experience of God. The most depraved reader of such an account is inwardly moved by it.

Therefore I know that I am perfectly safe in saying that no one who reads these words will deny *ever* having responded to truth or beauty or goodness. When you did respond, it was *an* experience of God. These are the doors through which God comes, and your temperament or approach to reality sometimes determines which door He uses. If you are a lover of truth He may get to you that way ; if you are a lover of beauty He may come that way; if neither of those mean much to you, He knows that there is still another way. He will come down His own secret stair.

But all these experiences are less than what the New Testament calls the experience of God in Christ. This must be stressed, lest men, questing for God, hearing us speak of beauty, truth, and goodness, reply : " Oh, is that all you mean ? " No, it is not all we mean, but it is a beginning to realise that God has spoken to us, has touched our life at this point and at that, and that finding Him is not finding a stranger, but One who has spoken to us already in many ways and is asking us to open ourselves more fully to His possessing.

Let us clarify the meaning of finding God by clearing away some misapprehensions.

We are not to look for an experience, we are to look for God—or better, to be found of Him. Many people have read or heard others speak of glowing experiences they have had. (And a warning will not be misunderstood that it is dangerously easy to talk up or write up such an experience.) Whereupon they say, "No such thing ever happens to me." They then either give up their quest deciding that their "temperament" is against it, or they pretend to an experience by trying to work themselves up emotionally. We are to recognise that God may not speak to us as He does to others, but we must let Him show Himself to us in *His way for us*. We must want *God*, not an experience of Him like other people's. So, often we watch one door and will not open another at which God is knocking. He has His own secret stairway into every life.

Then, we are not to measure the authenticity of an experience of God by emotion. Emotion is not the only valid thermometer by which we can take our spiritual temperature. There will be some moments when we are moved to the depths as, for example, when some preacher stirs our mind and heart by the beauty, passion and appeal of his words. But do you remember that morning when you started for work ten minutes earlier? You turned into a church. You prayed. You *almost* passed the church door, saying that you didn't feel like it, that in any case you would be thinking of all you had to do. Yet you went, and knelt, and coldly and dispassionately affirmed some great truth about God and life. You gave God your will, even though your heart was not in it. You gave him your obedience. You came away feeling prayer was unreal. Yet I believe God can do as much for you through that ten minutes as He can through the emotional experience of another occasion. By the assent of mind and will He can change your reactions to life; and, though you register no emotion, He is penetrating your spirit with His own, deeper and deeper, indeed at such a depth that you are incapable of judging just what He has accomplished; and the test is not whether you feel differently, but whether your reactions to life are different, whether you are easier to live with, whether your personality becomes reinforced with new power, whether a deep serenity is born in the depths of your nature, whether you develop a joy not merely the product of the circumstance of the moment, whether you begin to love others with a love that includes those who cordially dislike you.

Do we suppose that we could have shut up the poet Shelley in a room, like our bedroom for instance, at eight in the morning and tell him to write a poem by twenty-past? Do we think we could engineer those "feelings" which the poet experiences when the winds of inspiration are blowing and he is driven along gloriously with the urge to creative writing which resulted in poems like "The Cloud"?

But many a poet has gone to some quiet place and fulfilled a discipline. He has written words which were not good poetry. He has read the masters. He has meditated on this theme and that. He has come away after an hour " feeling " no different and perhaps tempted to give up writing. But he is becoming a poet more during such dull hours than during the hours of glorious inspiration. Those dull hours make the others possible. Later, given the stimulus, he reacts to it in some form of creative art which the world will treasure.

We shall not go to a room at eight o'clock and proceed to find God, if by finding God you mean feeling Sunday-nightish or what some of my friends call " bubbly." But if I undertake a discipline of seeking Him, and by His aid removing those things which stand between me and a full experience of Him, then though my feeling registers little I am in process of being found and I am becoming a Christian, becoming more and more ready to be made what He can make me, allowing Him often, below conscious and emotional levels of the mind, to change my reactions to life, and to help me so to hoist the sails that the winds of God can swing me to those havens of purpose which are in His plan for me.

I think for many the first finding of God is what our fathers called conversion. We feel that a hand is suddenly put upon our life; we are halted and turned round and sent forth in a new direction, where the purpose and glory of God instead of selfish-interest are the greater motives. We feel that the truest end of life is being caught up into His will and serving Him in terms of our daily job. Generally, at such a time, there is a tremendous sense of inner serenity, revitalising energy and a deep sense of well-being which quite often brings to the very body a new sense of health. One has seen people's facial expressions alter and their nerves find rest in this new orientation of life. But he who truly finds God is not content with that one crisis. He is seeking and finding God in everything, and although there will be peak experiences, yet even in the valleys, life can never be the same again. Nor does he ever end his seeking, for always there is more and more to find.

To find God means, moreover, a tremendous sense that in Him our sense of values will be justified and conserved—that whatever appearances are, and however jumbled up life may appear, however unjust, cruel, painful, calamitous the experiences of life may seem to be, to find Him means intuitively to know that love will triumph at last, justice will be upheld, pain will be explained and calamity fit into the pattern.

Life sometimes looks like a pile of the pieces of a jig-saw puzzle all heaped up together higgledy-piggledy, but when you have found God you have seen the picture on the inside of the lid. You know, by faith, that every piece will fit into its place at last and that the resultant picture will be perfect. Shall I be stretching the parable if I say that the picture on the inside of the lid is the face of Jesus Christ? " We know," said men of old, triumphantly, " we have seen the glory of God in the face of Jesus Christ." " Teach us to live so close to Thee," I find myself often praying, " that we may learn to love as those who believe that love which goes on loving will always win at last. For the honour of Jesus Christ our Lord, Amen."

II
WHERE SHALL I
BEGIN ?

WHERE SHALL I
BEGIN ?

LET us imagine a man engaged on a
serious quest for God. Let us
think of him as entirely sincere in his
desire to find God, willing to open all
the doors of his being which he can see,
to put away all compromises and excuses,
accept the pardon of God for the past,
and enter into a personal, conscious
communion, spirit with spirit, with One
recognised to be a fitting object of worship
and love, whose will he desires to do
and in Whom all his highest values are
conserved. Imagine such a man now
coming to us and saying, " Having thus
cleared my mind I want to go on. What
shall I do ? " It must be admitted that
the teaching of the Church has sometimes
been bewildering and vague in answering
this question. We have said, " Read
your Bible and say your prayers." We

may have said, " You will find God in service to others." We have said, " You will find God by coming to Church " ; and sometimes we have been more vague still and emphasised the undoubted fact that there are a hundred ways of finding God.

Perhaps some of us, myself included, ask for the impossible. We would really like a set of directions which would ensure success. A young man came to a friend of mine once with a note-book and pencil in his hand, saying, " Now then, I want to find God. Tell me what to do." My sympathies are very much with the young man. There is too much vague talk in religion. If a man asked the way to London it is not very much help to be told, " But there are lots of ways to London. You will find one, one day." Martineau asks just as direct a question— ' Where then is our God ? . . . You say, He is everywhere : then show me *anywhere* that you have met him. You declare him everlasting : then tell me any moment that he has been with you. You believe him ready to succour them that are tempted, and to lift those that are bowed down : then in what passionate hour did you subside into his calm grace ? in what sorrow lose yourself in his " more exceeding " joy ? These are the testing questions by which we may learn, whether *we too* have raised our altar to an " unknown God," and pay the worship of the blind ; or whether we commune with him " in whom we live and move and have our being." [1] Ought we not to face such questions and be much more decisive than this ? Is it not compelling logic that if God is seeking us, as we are believing He does, and if we are honestly and sincerely seeking Him and know what it is we are doing, there ought to be definite instructions to give a person so that he can put himself in the way of being found by God ? Are we only to say to him, " Well, put the sail up, the wind may blow one day and bring your ship into

[1] James Martineau, *Hours of Thought*, ii, 8.

port"; or "Keep on knocking on the door, somebody may open it some day"; or "Keep looking for God; it is a game of hide and seek, in which God hides and you seek, but one day you may be lucky." That, to me, seems all wrong.

Surely the beginning of the matter is an act of imaginative faith. To believe that God is there, just where we are, as real as the air we breathe, as available, as close; a loving and almighty Father who understands and is interested in the smallest detail of life. "He that cometh to God must believe that He is and that He is a rewarder of them that seek after Him."[1]

Let the seeker turn alone into some quiet place—I suggest a church—and spend ten minutes in silence by way of preparation, thinking of God as present, that infinite Spirit ever and always available throughout all His vast universe. Or, if it helps him more, let him make a mental picture of the Saviour standing

[1] Heb. xi, 6.

166

before him. If it helps him let him make a human picture of the Saviour in Eastern dress with kind, tender eyes and arms outstretched. Or, if it helps him more, let the seeker think of the Crucified.

Then let him kneel down and confess his sins, saying the words even if he feels no sense of presence. Then let him make a surrender of his life to God, asking God to help him not to keep anything back, telling God—if this be the truth—that his faith is very small and that he doesn't know what he does believe.

Then, after a silence, let him accept the forgiveness of God, telling himself that, because he is penitent, God puts all his sins behind His back and that therefore he must put them behind his. He must resolve on making such restitution as God will show him is necessary, and he may still have to suffer for past sins. But let him accept first the glorious truth of a relationship restored, a harmony recovered as though sin and indifference had never spoilt it. Let him not worry

even if he does not " feel " forgiven.
He has accepted the gift of a friendship
which will show him other sins and the
nature of all sin and sooner or later give
him a tremendous sense of release and
power. But first let him close with God's
offer of a new relationship whatever he
" feels " about it.

Then let him take hold of the thought
that the emphasis in future in his life
must be on God's friendship and power,
which he accepts as God's gift, and not
on his own will, though that will be needed
to the full, that in every situation God
will be with him, that God will never
forsake him or refuse to receive him back
again, and then let him go back to his
life believing that something has happened,
and acting as though it had happened,
relying constantly on God.

Let him keep at least ten minutes each
day to offer himself afresh to God, never
letting failure make him turn back. Let
him confide to some adequate friend his
quest and discovery. Let him join a

fellowship group—or start one—of those
who continually seek to know more and
more of God, and tell the members of
that Fellowship of the new life which he
has begun to live.[1]   And let him try, in
ways which God will reveal to him, to
bring another to the same point of
surrender. I am certain such a seeker
will not be disappointed.

He may find it of value to enter in his
diary some such oath of allegiance as I
print below and sign it. " On this day
I surrender my whole life to Jesus Christ.
Accepting His pardon and grace, from
henceforth by daily communion with
Him, I will seek to do His will in all
things. And, as He guides me, I will
make what restitution I can for the past,
and, having established fellowship, I will
try to bring others unto that experience
with Him which is changing me."

---

[1] I am aware, of course, of the value of the Fellowship
Group *before* one has any real experience of God. Many
have caught something by infection from the group. But
following that there must be for most the solitary encounter
with God and the act of surrender.

Let me add a paragraph on the richness which comes to life when we put God in the centre of our lives and try to see Him everywhere. Why, even in Old Testament days men found Him simply by the act of faith which believed that what they were seeking had happened—by an act of imaginative faith which thought of Him as there and present. " If I ascend up into heaven Thou art there. If I make my bed in the places of the dead, behold, Thou art there. If I take the wings of the morning and dwell in the uttermost parts of the sea, even there shall Thy hand lead me, and Thy right hand shall hold me." To some of those old Testament saints God was as real as the sunshine, and as present. Some of their ideas were mistaken, but their experience puts us to shame. If they won a battle, it was God. If they lost, God was punishing them. If the daylight seemed longer than usual, God had stayed the progress of the sun at the word of His servants. If the tide swept away their enemies, God had delivered them. If manna fell in the desert, God had sent it. Life was theocentric, God was in it all. The intellectual background of such a faith may need to be restated, but many of us are living very weak, anæmic spiritual lives, compared with those grand old men of the Old Testament.

Jesus entered into the heritage of a race of religious geniuses and carried religious genius to its perfect blossoming. It is the simple truth to say that everything He touched reminded him of God. If He saw a man sowing seed or ploughing a field, a shepherd folding his sheep, a woman sweeping the house, or mending garments, or making bread, or lighting a lamp; if He saw birds or lilies or sunsets or rain-storms: all things led His mind to God. And one feels, as one reads of Him in this situation and that, that God was in the centre of His life and in the centre of every situation that came to Him—that in His dealings with people the thought of God was never far away.

In God He lived and moved and had His being. In His beautiful mind all the paths led to God.

The way of Jesus is surely the way for us. We must begin to practise the presence of God by acts of imaginative faith. We must let our mind and heart accept the idea that God is present, that His life is sweeping through our own, that He is interested and concerned and even involved in all that we do, and say and think ; and we must train our minds so that all beautiful things make them fly to God, so that all sad things make us think of God and His comfort, so that all people in trouble are seen, as it were, through the eyes of God, so that all humour is God's goodness in cheering our lives. " But am I to think of God when I read *Punch* ? " someone asks, to which the answer was given, " Yes, He helps to write it." If we make the leap of faith which thinks of God as present in every circumstance speaking to us in the beauty and humour, sadness, of human life, challenging us in its pains and sorrows and calamities, so as to make us lay hold of things that do not pass away, then we shall find God everywhere and the whole earth will be full of His glory.

But some will feel that their idea of God is so vague that they cannot make such an unimaginative leap. Surely for them the best way—and perhaps it is easier for us all—is to think of Jesus. " Show us the Father," said Philip, " and it sufficeth." Jesus' answer was, " He that hath seen Me hath seen the Father." Perhaps the best answer, in a sentence, to the question, " How shall I find God? " is the answer, " Keep on looking at Jesus." In a way it was easy for Philip. There was a face to see with physical eyes, words to hear with physical ears. There was a life to watch, lived out before them by the Son of God, till it dawned upon them that what they were watching was God manifested in the flesh. Having found Him they had found and seen God. A little band of men, by the grace of God, were received into a friendship. Their Friend was tempted just as they were, yet He never fell. Their Friend knew what fear was, yet it never swayed Him from His purposes. Their Friend knew the petty irritations of life, the way life has of thrusting up its cares before the mind ; yet before those deep, clear eyes, worry slunk away ashamed, seeing in their depths the horrid reflection of itself. Their Friend was jostled by the crowd, continually besieged, never allowed a moment's peace if the crowd could find Him. They themselves in His place would have been jarred beyond words. Their nerves would have frayed under the strain. They got irritable even on His behalf. " Send the multitudes away ! " was their cry. But " He was a refuge for every hunted life." He had time for every one. He was never too busy. He was never fretted. He was never hysterical. He was always ready to receive men, and listen to them, and show His belief in them—always eager to heal their souls and minds and bodies, always speaking words of authority and pardon, of strength and graciousness.

Time came when their Friend was suspected, was deserted—yes, even by themselves. Time came when He was tried, mocked, scourged . . . crucified. Yet He never stopped loving ; and from the depth of His agony He breathed a prayer of forgiveness, and made friends with a dying felon on the cross next to His own. Dead ? Oh, yes, He was dead—just like other men. No doubt there were plenty of people in Jerusalem who used those four words—" just like other men." The disciples, may be, used them themselves—" just like other men." But one morning the dawn broke fresh and gloriously. There was a wild story told by a woman. There was a race to a tomb. There was a Presence here, there, everywhere, and they began to ask one another a question—" What if this Friend happen to be God ? "

We still have the haunting desire to see Him and need the spiritual equivalent of what they had in physical terms. Our problem then becomes that of finding Jesus.[1]

> I wish that His hands had been placed on my head,
> That His arms had been thrown around me,
> And that I might have seen His kind look when He said,
> Let the little ones come unto Me.

We grown-ups can hardly sing the verse of that kiddies' hymn without a filling of the eyes and a lump in the throat. If only we could be as *sure* of Him as that. It seems almost cruel if such a radiant Personality, the only One in whom all our dreams come true, the only Master of Life, who lived life as God dreamed it instead of as we know it, moved over the stage of history and then passed out of humanity's ken. For we know that if we could go out and live for a week in His physical presence, life

[1] Much of what follows in this chapter was broadcast in the National Wireless Programme and is reproduced by permission of the British Broadcasting Corporation.

would be a different thing. We shouldn't want to do and say the things for which we hate ourselves. And in six months we should be utterly changed by that transforming friendship.

It is the claim of Christianity that that physical presence became unnecessary, but that its spiritual reality is possible to everybody. Indeed I believe that Christianity never means what it might mean to a man until he knows for himself the reality of a personal relationship with Christ.

Ritual is valuable and beautiful. So are music and architecture. Creeds have a place in helping us express our thoughts about God. So have intellectual discussions. Organisation is essential that Christian work may be done efficiently; but none of these things change men's lives, and none is essential to the life of the soul. Unless we find Jesus for ourselves and have a living communion with Him, our religion becomes either a secular affair altogether, a dreary carrying

177

M

out of certain forms, or else a "trying to be good," God vaguely in the background, being our helper, instead of our glad, complete acceptance of the offer of a friendship which has power in it to make us what we most want to be.

I am not blind to the fact that to say we can really find Jesus to-day is to make a stupendous claim. It is to claim that John Smith, in broad daylight, directly, and on normal levels of the mind, can get into immediate communion with that radiant Spirit who, clothed then in a physical body, walked and talked in Galilee two thousand years ago. No wonder faith sometimes fails ! No wonder the sceptic asks, " How do you know it is Himself, and not some sub-jective illusion of your own mind ? " No wonder that, even for the devout, the gulf between our hurrying, hectic streets and the quiet Voice that called to men and women in the fields and woods of Galilee, seems wider than faith can span, deeper than desire can bear !

We must not turn away impatiently from such questions. There is an answer as scientific as any answer in the realm of the mystical can be. I cannot prove to you by logic that you can find Him, but I think I can prove to you that there is no reason on His side why you shouldn't.

First of all there can be no doubt that that radiant Personality survived death. Whatever our theory of the Resurrection may be, Christ's survival—the survival of all that is essentially Christ—is the only thing that accounts for the rescue of eleven men from utter and complete despair. If the Resurrection is another ghost story, it is a new thing in ghost stories which turns abject terror into flaming courage, and cowards into heroes and martyrs. It drove ordinary shrinking men like ourselves, as Miss Kirkland says, to go shouting a message to audiences as derisive as some men are to-day, a message punished with stripes and crosses and red-jowled beasts, yet persisting, indomitable, on and on down the echoing centuries, until a pagan world was conquered by a handful of Jewish fishermen, and a great Church raised its pinnacles to heaven, to enshrine that message flung to the wind on the first Pentecost, " Jesus Christ is alive."

First, He establishes contact through their senses. Gradually He carried them beyond the need of the senses, and convinced them, against all their preconceptions, of His survival. If this be true, at what point in history did He cease to manifest Himself? No one has ever suggested that there was such a point. The claim that He is not findable is a denial of history, and it is a denial of the experience of some of the finest men and women the world has ever seen, who, for the sake of the truth of that experience, have sallied forth on the most desperate exploits in the spiritual history of the world. Many of them have never seen visions or heard voices, but through questing faith and adventurous prayer there has come to them such an inward reinforcement of personality which no adverse circumstance can undermine, such a serenity of heart which nothing can invade, such an infectious gaiety which no grief or depression can quell, such an outgoing love to others, including even critics and enemies—their lives have been so changed, changed as none other has ever changed lives save Jesus of Nazareth, that the most reasonable way of explaining their experience is to assert that they have found Him for themselves.

But, of course, it will not content us to know that the experience is reasonable, or that others have found Him. Can *we* find Him ? We want to find Him for ourselves. What are the conditions ?

If we are really seeking Him must there not be a personal submission as well as a faith ready to expect and adventure ? We often sing the hymn containing the words :

But sweeter far Thy face to see,
And in Thy presence rest.

But I know my own heart at least well enough to realise that an encounter with Jesus would be surgical before it was restful. We say, " Can we really find Him to-day ? " You ask to see His face. Are you *willing* for those eyes to burn through to your secret sins and inward rottenness ? Are you *willing* to have your whole life confronted by the kindest but the most inexorable eyes in the world ? His love is full of compassion, but there is steel in it too. It is a love that never lets us go, but a love which never lets us off.

If His presence isn't real to many of us, is it partly what the New Testament calls " unbelief " which, even in the days of His flesh, robbed His friendship of its transforming possibilities to many ? I do not mean an intellectual unbelief. That, if sincere, He will honour, since He seems to have been slow to demand from His disciples intellectual assent to propositions. I mean a refusal of His way of life. Am I really wanting to find Him or am I wanting Him with half my nature, while, all the time, the other half is saying, " No," or " Not yet," and is hugging to itself some secret unclean lust or shame ? That is the trouble with many of us. We only half want to find Him, lest we have to give up the sins we have grown to love.

There must surely be willingness for that personal closure with Christ, a willingness to receive Him into every part of the life, and a closure which the soul dreads and yet longs for, desires and yet puts off. I think this is His condition, and we can only have Him on His terms.

Granting this, the remainder is within the reach of every man. Are you *willing* to be alone for fifteen minutes each day, preferably when the mind is not overtired, dropping into a church, for instance on your way from, or to, work ; sacrificing that mid-morning cup of coffee or that after-tea smoke ? No life is so full that this is impossible. Are you *willing* in that fifteen minutes to make an adventure of expectant faith, not looking for some definite *experience*, especially an emotional experience, *not seeking an experience*, but seeking Christ and letting Him come to you in His own way? I suggest that on some days we should read one of the great hymns, or one of the Gospel narratives, following Ruskin's advice—" to be present as if in the body at some recorded act in the life of the Redeemer." On another day we might pray through the great prayers of others, or write out a prayer of our own to help us keep that wandering mind on the quest we are making, and then sitting silently, with the body relaxed, and doing what I can only call "looking at Him." A heart lifted up in adoration and a will bent to daily obedience will not go unrewarded.

The world needs nothing as it needs, in every phase of life, people who are trying out Christ's way of life, and who have an ever-deepening experience of

184

Him—who are advertisements of what His way is and what it does. For, indeed, how can we expect to see Christ reign in the great world's life if He does not reign in our own? Are not the strife, unrest, and evil in the world but a magnification of the state of our own hearts?

If you seek Him, then, you will find what men and women found who lived in His presence long years ago, that Christ's way is a way *through*, and that all other ways are " dead ends." You will find that you love the things He loves, and hate the things in yourself and in the world which He hates. You will find that all life is filling with new meaning, new purpose, new beauty; that your old conflicts, depressions, self-loathings, have slunk away like morning mists before the coming of the sun. It is not so much that you have found Him; it is that at last, in your hectic, hurried life, you have given Him a chance to do what He has been trying to do all your conscious days, to find you.

Let me add a word on the use of the imagination, for at the beginning of the chapter I spoke about an act of *imaginative* faith. The imagination, we must remember, is not only a faculty by which we may conjure up something that has no existence in reality, but by which we may apprehend a reality which cannot be seen. If it is scientific to use the faculty of sight to make sure of the presence of a visible person, why is it unscientific to use the faculty of imagination to realise an unseen presence ? It is not unscientific. Science uses imagination more than she is ready to admit. A man sees an apple fall. He imagines a law which he cannot see. He tests it in experiment, and he finds confirmation. Thousands have imagined a Presence, tested it in experience, found that something marvellous and transforming has happened to them, that very same " something " which happened to men who were transformed by the presence of Jesus when He moved and taught in Galilee.

If they imagined something that was false or not there, their experience would, in time, give it the lie. In this way we have been compelled to relinquish our childhood's faith in fairies. Spiritual reality is reached, not through argument, but through experience, and experience needs a venture of faith—a faith which may begin in, and be constantly strengthened by, the faculty of imagination which is, in its own sphere, as reputable as sight.

> The love of Jesus, what it is,
> None but His loved ones know.

But *they* know.

One of my friends formed the habit of imagining that, when he walked down a certain street on the way to business, Jesus was walking with Him. Now he is sure. If, contrary to custom, he has any occasion to walk down the street at another time or with a friend a strange hush falls upon his spirit. Someone else is there, too. Imagination was a doorway into a living faith.

So many of us, as it seems to me, are hammering on a door that is open, seeking feverishly for someone who is there waiting to reveal Himself. I am reminded, by the experiences of many who talk to me, of a woman of whom Dr. Maltby once wrote, who was much troubled by the question, " How can I find God ? " And once or twice she had this dream. She dreamed that she was standing in front of a thick plate-glass window. As she looked at it she seemed to see God on the other side, dimly and distantly. She hammered on the window hoping to catch His attention, but there was no response. Growing desperate she called to Him, and then screamed to try and catch His attention. At the height of her desperation she heard the quiet voice of One who was standing near her, and this is what the voice said : " What are you making such a noise for ? There is nothing between us."

I want to suggest that this is the matter with hundreds of us. Given that we

have cleared our minds of insincerity,
that we are not seeking Him with half
our mind and shutting doors against
Him by hanging on to our sins or refusing
to put right our human relationships.
Is it not the truth to say that we are
seeking someone who is here, that what
we need to do is to put out the hand of
our spirit and touch Him? To have an
imaginative faith, to believe that He is
here at this moment, loving us, bending
over us, interested in us. Let us steep
our mind in the thought of His presence,
train our mind so that all things and
people that touch our life are linked up
in our mind with God. Let us make the
act of faith by which we believe in the
reality and presence of the One we seek,
and go out for a week putting it into
practice, testing it in experience, proving
it in our changed lives and on the very
word of Jesus, " according to our faith,
it shall be done unto us."

Will you allow me to press upon you
this personal closure with Christ? Don't

just say, " Yes, I'll think about it later."
Don't say, " Well, after the holidays
perhaps, or after this examination, or
after this business deal." Do not even
merely say, " I really will be a better
man or woman; I'll go to church, I'll
read the Bible, I'll begin to pray." Do
not say, " I can't promise again, I've
broken my promises too often " ; " I can't
promise to be consistent " ; " I've grown
old and fatal in habit ; it's all right for
young people perhaps, but not for me,
not for me."

If you feel like saying " not for me,"
you are in the mood when Christ can do
most. Jesus had three great words,
Dr. George Jackson reminds us, " Least,"
" Last," and " Lost," and He said, " The
least should be greatest, the last should
be first, and the lost should be found."
You are making the wrong emphasis—
" I," " I," " I." Through the New
Testament runs another note. " He is
able." " He is able." " He is able."

Will you go to some quiet place or

creep up to your room, or go out under the stars alone? He is nearer to you than any figure of speech can describe. He will receive you. He will understand you. He will believe in you. He will know what to do with you. He will tell you where to begin, and you will go back to a life that is quite different because He has found you, and you have found Him. You will find Him everywhere, both within and without, and for you the whole earth will be full of His glory. For where He toucheth there is healing. Where He beckoneth, there the light shines. And where He dwelleth, there is peace.

III
CAN'T I FIND GOD IN
SERVICE TO MEN ?

CAN'T I FIND GOD IN
SERVICE TO MEN?

A DISTINGUISHED doctor of divinity in my Church once got rather impatient with a conference of ministers who had met to discuss the question, "How can I find God?" It seemed to him a confession of failure that ministers should discuss such a question. He directed us to discard our quests and "find God in social service and in uncompromising opposition to every form of injustice and cruelty."

Let us admit at once that in service to humanity many people have been stimulated to seek a personal relationship with God. Let us admit an equal truth, that no man will keep his experience of having found God who does not go out and help others to find the same experience. The spirit of God is like electricity in this, that it will not come in where it can't get out. You can touch a bare cable carrying a thousand volts if you are perfectly insulated. To seek an experience of God merely for selfish ends will effectually insulate us from receiving living power.

But would it not be very dangerous to say to a seeker after God, " Serve and you shall find " ? Would you send a seeker after God into our slums, or to work amongst immorality, drunkenness and vice, or indeed to face the pride, indifference and selfishness of some of the so-called upper classes ? I suggest that so much is demanded from those who would serve that nothing but a living experience of God will prove sufficient to keep them at it and at the same time empower them to do it as it ought to be done.

A missionary doctor who had seen service in China once told me of a young girl who set sail for the mission-field with great ardour and enthusiasm.

The final stages of her journey had to be made in a crowded steamer which slowly crept up the swirling waters of a great Chinese river. For a certain period she had to stand among a crowd of Chinese who thronged her on every hand. She was small of stature. A huge Chinaman suffering from discharging ulcers was so close to her that she felt the discharge drop on the thin material of her blouse and soak through to her shoulder. A great nausea permeated her whole being. When she landed she was in tears. The kindly doctor met her and inquired what was the matter. She told him she had made a great mistake. She hated the Chinese and could not bear to stay and live amongst them. Very wisely and tenderly the missionary sent her away into retreat. The burden of her prayer was this : " O God, either you must show me your glory or I must go home." During the days that followed she found God. She realised all that God had suffered at *her* hands ; all He had done for her. She came down from that retreat and began a life spent in most devoted service to the Chinese people.

I write without any conscious cynicism when I say that I have seen people, impatient with our emphasis on the prior need of personal surrender, set out on this service and on that with tremendous gusto—and be beaten down by the forces arrayed against them. To change the figure, such folk come home bankrupt. There wasn't enough in the bank of love with which to meet the terrific expenditure. The reaction from such an experience can often be judged by the blank expression of despair which the face wears or by the cynicism which sometimes follows such failure. Even the disciples did not find God in the service of village folk who rejected their message. Bitterly disappointed and disgusted they demanded fire from heaven. Their love had run out.

I am reminded here of a story Dr. T. R. Glover tells of an agnostic friend of his who set out to save a drunkard in order to prove that a man's habits could be transformed without the aid of religion. He admitted that it was a filthy job. The man was so weak that he was utterly unable to pass a public house unless someone had hold of his arm, and the only way of saving him was to give him continuous comradeship, take him for walks, sit up with him at night, and stand by him all the time. If his guardian went up to London for a day he immediately went out and got drunk. Still the experiment went forward, and the optimistic unbeliever declared that he would stick to his friend and save him without any Christian assistance. One day Dr. Glover met him and said: "What about your drunken friend?" "Ah," was the reply, "I was getting on fairly well with the job when a lot of rough people in red jerseys arrived with an atrocious brass band. Somehow these repulsive fellows got hold of him. I don't know exactly what happened, but they seem to have made him kneel down and pray. Anyhow he can walk past a pub by himself now." In that story the secrets of many failures are disclosed. Like all the Churches the Salvation Army has its faults. I have always been impressed by the fact that it never ceases to offer men Christ and will not let them engage in Christian service until they have found Him.

We are all moved when we read the words of Rabindranath Tagore :

There is Thy footstool and there rest Thy feet, where live the poorest, and lowliest, and lost.

When I try to bow to Thee, my obeisance cannot reach down to the depth where Thy feet rest among the poorest, and lowliest, and lost.

Pride can never approach to where Thou walkest in the clothes of the humble among the poorest, and lowliest, and lost.

My heart can never find its way to where Thou keepest company with the companionless among the poorest, the lowliest, and the lost.

But my heart will find its way in those dread places where men need most to be served only when it has been redeemed, or is in process of being redeemed, and when it has learnt at the foot of the Cross the secret of a love that never lets go and that flames with an undying fire because it is fed by that unseen fuel which only comes from a new relationship with God.

Let the other side be stated. Many have gone forth to serve and have seen the need of the world. That need has stabbed them to the heart and they have been driven back on a search for God themselves, and, having given themselves to Him, returned with new resources and added zest to their task. But, in my experience, as many have had nervous breakdowns. Few can stand the strain without the resources which those know who are in a vital relationship with God.

As Matthew Arnold says in his sonnet, " East London " :

I met a preacher there I knew and said :
    " Ill and o'erworked, how fare you in this
      scene ?"
    " Bravely," he said, " for I of late have been
Much cheered with thoughts of Christ, the Living
      Bread."

Nor do I criticise the service rendered to the needy by those who have no experience of God. It is magnificent and God surely honours it. It is splendid philanthropy if it is not Christian service.

What I am saying is that in my view it is dangerous to tell a man he will find God by serving men. He is more likely either to find the Devil or return possessed by cynicism and loathing and despair. Or he will hide—as thousands of earnest " Christian " people in the Churches are hiding—from the relentless demands of Christ by doing His service.

But God does not want their service so much as He wants to find them and bring them home. The prodigal did good service no doubt in the far country. He may indeed have become chairman of the incorporated society for the prevention of cruelty to pigs and served on innumerable committees, all having a worthy purpose. But if so he didn't bluff his father that all was well. He didn't even bluff himself. For he came to himself, and when that happened he immediately arose and came to his father.

Forgive the direct word. Do you think when you stand before the great white throne that you can bluff God by telling Him you were a trustee's treasurer, or a missionary collector, or a Sunday school teacher or church officer? Will God be satisfied because you have been a Rotarian, or an Oddfellow, a Mason, a Forester, or a Buffalo? He doesn't want our good works if they are a substitute for ourselves or an evasion of His appeal.

'Tis through Thy love alone we gain
   The pardon of our sin;
The strictest life is but in vain,
   Our works can nothing win;
That none should boast himself of aught
But own in fear Thy grace hath wrought
What in him seemeth righteous.

HOW CAN I FIND GOD?

Wherefore my hope is in the Lord,
    My works I count but dust,
I build not there, but on His word,
    And in His goodness trust.
Up to His care *myself* I yield,
He is my tower, my rock, my shield,
And for His help I tarry.

IV
CAN'T I FIND HIM IN THE SERVICES AND SACRAMENTS OF THE CHURCH?

CAN'T I FIND HIM IN THE SERVICES AND SACRAMENTS OF THE CHURCH?

WE need not spend much time on the question, " Can we find God in the services of the Church ? " Surely the answer is " Yes," if we look for Him in the right way. The subject gives me the opportunity of saying that we ought more definitely to make the quest of God the definite motive of every service. There is just a danger lest a Sunday evening service should become a subtle form of entertainment. Not that it is wrong to enjoy the anthem or the corporate singing or even the sermon; but they should all be means to an end, not ends in themselves. The Free Churches have probably made a mistake in attaching too great importance to the sermon. So, in some Free Churches the ideal of *worship* is somewhat obscure; but every minute of the service should be arranged with the definite purpose of getting the people who attend it into living touch with God.

If a man wants to see the stars, it may be that some astronomer will allow him to use a telescope. If he is a wise observer he will not spend a great deal of time admiring the telescope, nor will he spend much time in criticising it. His aim will be to use it; to look not at it, but through it, so that he may see the stars. And he has no right to criticise it unless, after he has done all he can do, the stars, on a clear night, are not brought nearer to him. The same is true of a Church service. We should not be looking at it either in the spirit that is content only to say, " That was a beautiful anthem," or " That was a poor sermon." At every point in the service our spirit should be set to worship, to look *through* the means provided and see God. And we have no right to criticise the service unless, after we have brought all our faith and longing and desire, the service fails to bring God nearer to us.

At the same time I would like to make a plea for beautiful and reverent services, services throbbing with *reality*. There is something in the beauty and dignity of the Anglican service that greatly appeals to me. Further, the building is generally a beautiful one. That of itself helps many of us to find God. And yet how often the service is spoiled. I took my two boys recently to an Anglican service. I was horribly disappointed. I wanted them to catch the sense of reverence, the hush, the awe, the dignity which I have so often found helpful in the Church of England. But the voice of the priest intoning, the choice of the Psalms for the day, Psalms which had nothing to do with life as people live it, the ten-minute sermon read word for word from a manuscript, how utterly unreal it all seemed. Frankly, with Donald Hankey, I don't want to sing Psalms which thank God " who smote

209

O

many nations and slew mighty kings; Sihon king of the Amorites, and Og king of Bashan."[1] I am not interested in Og king of Bashan. And I wondered what the sensible-looking business man on one side of me and the faded little woman in front of me really made of these alleged aids to worship. I could not work up an interest in the long chapter from the Book of Kings which a curate with a terrible nasal twang read as his first lesson, because, presumably, it was *set*. Why *do* we waste people's time for worship by repulsive stories of "bloody revenge, vindictive prayers, childish conceptions of God and materialistic conceptions of salvation"? Why must the anthem—beautifully sung, be it said—contain the words "a thousand shall fall at thy side and ten thousand at thy right hand, but it shall not come nigh thee"? What does the mother of the boy killed in France think of that? And why do we make people sing

[1] Psalm cxxxv, 10, 11.

hymns about being weary of earth?
Why do we choose hymns that make
Jesus seem effeminate and sentimental?
Why do we choose hymns of utter
consecration and ask a thousand people
to say words they cannot mean?

> Jesus, I my Cross have taken,
> All to leave and follow Thee.

Why do we make people recite Creeds,
hardly a sentence of which they can say
without making mental reservations,
making words mean what they don't
say, and pretending to a spurious and
false uniformity by a species of intellectual
dishonesty? " I know the Creeds," said
a young officer to Canon Hannay (George
Birmingham), " but that is not what I
want. I want to know *what you really
think*." " What does ' I believe in the
resurrection of the body ' mean? " asked
a young Indian student of the present
writer. " I suppose it means ' I believe
in the survival of personality '," said I.
" *Then why don't you say so?* " was his

challenging reply. " You must not interpret too literally," we say. But it doesn't seem unreasonable to ask that, even in religion, words should mean what they say. Oliver Wendell Holmes asks in one of his books what would become of the science of mathematics if two meant two to one man, twenty-two to another, a hundred and two to another. The result would be unthinkable confusion. I suggest that the theology of the man in the street is in a similar muddle and that it is largely the Church's fault. As Dr. Oman says, our people " wander in the perpetual twilight among shadowy ghosts of former faiths which they will not expel and cannot embrace." We are teaching our people to hug unreality to their bosom and stifle their intellectual consciences under musty old forms, and then we wonder that their " beliefs " are worthless to them in the hour of real need and calamity. The man in the street more than suspects that we ourselves recognise that many "infallibilities" have been overthrown; yet Sunday by Sunday he hears—if he goes to Church—the impossible method being attempted of trying to re-establish them by continual affirmation in archaic language which we ourselves only believe in a sense quite different from the normal meanings of the words used and in a sense entirely different from that intended by those who first wrote the words down. A chemist who refuses to believe in the new-fangled theories of electrons and protons and who still believes Dalton's atomic theory may possibly be respected. But a chemist who pretended to maintain the "uniformity of teaching" by using the word atom and making the mental reservation that by atom he meant something quite different would be called a fool, and not even an honest fool. The language of the Creeds comes perilously near the same kind of wangling, and the Anglican service cries aloud for drastic revision on the plea for reality.

Just after the war Lieutenant Crump
of Cambridge put a good deal of what
I want to say into verse. I hope he will
forgive my quoting them. I do not
know where they appeared. I only have
them in a notebook. He was lying
beneath the chestnut trees one glorious
summer morning. The air was full of
the scent of flowers and resonant with
the hum of bees. He says :

I wondered, too, if God could not be found
In better ways than lying on the ground
And dreaming of Him . . . .
. . . . So I fetched my coat,
Fastened a stiff white collar round my throat,
Put sixpence in my pocket, brushed my hair,
Knocked out my pipe, wondered what hat to wear,
Wasted five minutes in a fruitless search
For a clean pair of gloves, and went to church.
There was a crowd of women in big hats
And jingling jewellery ; men with spats
And frock coats, each the other's imitator,
All come to show respect to their Creator.
I stood and waited in the streets outside
Until those worshippers had occupied
The pews they pay for,
And then with swelling chords that rent the air
The organist proclaimed that he was there.
And then we stood to hear the choir boys sing
The barbarous poems of a Hebrew king.

They then sat down to enjoy their well-earned
    slumbers
While someone read a chapter out of Numbers.

.   .   .   .   .

Their worship's over; God returns to Heaven
And stays there till next Sunday at eleven.

Is it not far too true a caricature of
modern worship? Just as the people
mentioned in the first chapter of Isaiah
mistook ritual for reality, and were
content to watch the incense rise without
a thought of real prayer, were content
to see a bullock slain without the
sacrifice of heart, so are we not content
to let the form of worship be sufficient
while our real devotion is withheld?
God remains far off and unreal, and the
definite dynamic for daily life which
religion could give is never realised.
The repetition of familiar religious acts
goes on while the deeps of the soul
remain untouched and the adoration of
the heart is withheld. And many a man
in his hour of so-called worship feels
like a fish out of water, feels a strange
sense of being in an unreal atmosphere,

because nothing in his worship touches the life he lives every day. He seeks for the living God in vain.

That much devotion is insincere then is partly the fault of the Churches who make no effort to touch the things which touch the life of the average man. It still means nothing to God, as it would mean nothing to you if you were God, that men and women should sing praises they do not feel, ask for half-understood favours, pretend an insincere humility while all the time their life is a thing apart, untouched, unchallenged; and while the evil of the day walks the streets naked and unashamed, God says again in this our day, " I abhor your vain oblations."

How often, indeed, a man in real need must come to church, find a seat and be turned out of it by an enraged seatholder, sit through prayers which mean nothing to him or whose familiarity makes it an effort for them to become the expression of his own need, listens to a lesson read because it is set to be read, and sits through a sermon on some obscure subject *and catches never a sight of Jesus who wants him and wants to help him along the coming road, and wants his allegiance in the fight against evil.* He may never come again. The worship of the Church must touch the *life* men live. Christ is not only the Christ of stained-glass windows but the Companion on the dusty road. Christ is too often wrapped up in the dress which the Church has made for Him. He is obscured by the words which teach what He is. To many He becomes a ghost. The Christ of the Churches is not conceived as the Companion of the Road. The Christ of the Intellect is not conceived as the Christ of the Heart. The Christ of History fails to become the Christ of Experience. People are still hungry for God. How often we offer them husks !

But the Free Church service can be just as unreal in the help it offers us to bring

us into vital touch with God. One
remembers with a shudder the kind of
building in which some services are held.
Let honour be paid to those who have
had very little money with which to
build and have done the best they could.
But in some cases the lack of money
has not been the problem, yet the
building erected has not had a beautiful
line about it or a beautiful thing in it.
So far can the protest of our Protestant-
ism and Nonconformity carry us ! The
whole service in Free Churches so often
can only be characterised by one word. It
is slovenly. The choir dressed in various
styles of apparel and millinery sits in
the most prominent place in the building,
whispers at odd moments and is not
above sweet-sucking during the sermon.
The preacher, dressed in the same clothes
in which afterwards he will eat his dinner,
smoke his pipe and go to sleep in his chair,
enters the pulpit. His prayer is an
abrupt haranguing of the congregation,
though the words are addressed to God.

One cannot help feeling that he would collect himself with greater care in order to enter the presence of his doctor. It is incredible that he would talk like that if he really thought he was in the presence of the Holy God; if he really thought it was his task to lift his fellow-worshippers into that august Presence. Then, having meandered and wandered in so-called prayer here and there and probably mis-stated the political situation, he will proceed with a service, the success of which almost entirely depends on his own health, physical, mental and spiritual. Late-comers will be directed to their seats by jovial sidesmen who, between two lines of the hymn they happen to be singing, will enquire after the worshippers' health and that of their families, and we have the following exciting dialogue :

Steward (bellowing) : But ah ! this faithless heart of mine,

(Then, in a loud whisper)—How's your mother ?

(Continuing to sing) Forgive me, O my Friend Divine,

(Continuing the conversation) My word, isn't it 'ot this morning ?—

and various other similar interpolations in a hymn which is supposed to express the deepest aspirations of the human personality. The announcement of the collection seems the signal for a general buzz of conversation which one would be an optimist to suppose had any reference to corporate worship. The sermon in most Free Churches is above the average Anglican effort, but that is not saying a very great deal, and an arresting delivery is a comparatively rare phenomenon.

I shall be told that such a picture is a caricature of Free Church worship. I have no wish to caricature or exaggerate. I have been present repeatedly at such services and taken part in them with a sinking heart. No word of what is written above is not based on actual observation. I am not surprised at poor congregations, for I do not know any experience in life so utterly depressing as, say, the morning service at some of our huge, barn-like down-town chapels, services without a scrap of colour, beauty, dignity, reverence, appeal or "liveness" about them. And I honour deeply those laymen who "keep the old place going," and I wonder what in their inmost mind they really suppose is being achieved. I honour even more those heart-broken ministers who "labour" (an apposite word!) there, who would be criticised out of the place if they introduced responsive prayers, or hung a cross in some conspicuous place, or wore a gown, or robed the choir, or had early communion, or threw up the morning service in favour of a "group" of keen young people who are as hungry for reality as they are. So the dreary, ugly services go on, attended by some out of compassion for the minister, by others out of loyalty for "the old place," by others out of sheer habit and custom, by others out of a half-conscious supposition

221

that God is squared by such attendance and the conscience kept in quiet comfort.

" When the Monday came," says Mark Rutherford of the peasants in *The Revolution in Tanner's Lane*, " they went to their work in the marshes and elsewhere, and lived their blind lives under grey skies, with nothing left in them of the Sunday save the recollection of a certain routine performed which might one day save them from some disaster . . . It was not, however, a reality to them. The wheelwright and his wife, and the six labourers with their wives, listened as oxen might listen, wandered home along the lanes heavy-footed like oxen, with heads toward the ground, and went heavily to bed." What a true picture that is of many of the services of Nonconformity ! What a contrast is the radiant experience Christ offers and which is reflected, for instance, in the Book of Acts. Is it any wonder that the Churches produce the kind of man who is so hard to win, who is so familiar with religion and so far from God ; who attends services and committees, but has no real experience? We have taught him to be satisfied with unreality. We have softened down the hard sayings of Christ, not demanded self-surrender, not offered a transforming experience. No wonder that Karl Barth writes : " The man whom the Church with much labour attains, the pious man self-justified by his piety, is the last strong obstacle this side the action of God."

Religion was the greatest enemy of Christianity in the days of Christ. Against it His strongest invective was hurled. Religion without reality is still the greatest enemy of vital Christianity, greater than materialism itself. The religion of the kind of man of whom Barth writes is a fake, a spurious substitute, a dismal lie, often covered by much " service " and committee work, but without any experience of Christ at its centre. It is the form without the fire. It is the most dangerous of all spiritual drugs. It puts the soul to sleep and makes it dream that it is religious. Let such a man awake, for the harlots will go into the Kingdom before him. Whatever they are they are not deceived.

Criticism of Church services there will always be. But the thing that hurts is that the severest criticism comes from the finer elements in human nature. Men are asking, " How can I find God ? " and the Church service so rarely helps them. That rarity is illustrated, for instance, among other ways by the success of the Oxford Group Movement. Men who have attended " services " all their lives have said, " I've found reality at last."

If only the wayfarer dropping in to any Church service was enwrapped with the atmosphere of friendship, was made to feel by the psychic atmosphere of the worshippers that this was a place where people prayed—if only the living Christ were always offered in a service in which every part pointed to Him, and every heart was lifted to Him so that He became savingly real to all within the walls— then our churches would be thronged each Sunday. For men and women who are sick of the squabbles of denominationalism, confused by the wrangling of theologians, hurt by the glib slovenliness of the chapel, and chilled by the cold formalities of the church, are desperately hungry for the Bread of Life, almost frantic in their search for a real way of life, for the secret of the mastery of the art of living, and they know from their own failures that only One can help them and they know the Churches pretend to function in His name. But it is not that they will not come to Him that they may find life. It is that when they do come to our services He is obscured instead of offered. We ought to try and remember that the only value in the

225

P

existence of the Church is to offer Christ to those who seek Him.[1]

When we turn to the Holy Communion there is a difference. There, in a posture of reverence, accompanied by words with few archaisms and carefully chosen, the seeker is offered Christ in the sacred elements. Unfortunately in the Anglican Church he cannot attend such a service until he has been confirmed, so it is useless to invite the outsider to look for Christ in the Holy Communion as celebrated by the Anglican Church. He must be well inside before he is allowed the free grace of God as mediated through this Sacrament.

I think the Free-Churchman or person unattached to any Church should accept the invitation frequently given in Free Churches to " all who love Christ and seek to follow His way of life " and reverently join in this service and take the sacred elements. He need not be

[1] That I do not disparage the possibilities of public worship or minimise the obligation of Christian people to attend services is clearly seen by the incident on p. 233.

sound in doctrine before he does this.
The men who sat round the table in the
upper room were not questioned as to
their doctrines. They were not confirmed
in their beliefs. They each pledged
themselves in loyalty to Christ even
to the breaking of their bodies and the
shedding of their blood. Whatever else
the service means it is a *sacramentum*,
an oath of allegiance, and to come to the
table to take that oath and in a true
desire to find God, is enough. The
philosophy of the symbolism can be
considered later.[1]

Some of us feel sometimes a longing,
greater than we can put into words, to
see Christ's face, to hear His word, to
feel His hand on our shoulder. It cannot
be, and perhaps it is better so. But there
is a precious symbol which reminds us
of Him in a special way. It is a piece
of bread and a cup of wine. If you
have lost your dearest, it is not a pillar
in the cemetery that you cherish most,

---

[1] A book on the Sacraments is promised in this series.

or perhaps the books he wrote or the signature of his name on the annals of fame; it is his Bible or his photograph, or a letter to you. The name of Jesus is written on the scroll of fame. He says, " Do not forget Me." True the world will never be able to forget Him, but He offers to those who seek Him a precious symbol, quite willing that we should join the band of disciples round His table. The symbol is as precious and intimate as a photograph, a Bible, a letter. " When you eat this bread and drink this cup, think of Me." There is no theory to be believed first, though the devout partaker will constantly find new and deeper meanings in the symbol. Do not be deterred because you " do not like ritual." Do not wait to become an orthodox member of an official Church. To those who love Him He says, " Do this in remembrance of Me," and those who do it enter into an ineffable mystery. Something happens greater than the recollection of a hushed room in far-off Jerusalem many years ago. Jesus Himself is there, and in that Presence the soul knows it has found God.

V
CAN'T I FIND GOD
IN NATURE ?

CAN'T I FIND GOD
IN NATURE?

I SHALL not deal with this theme at length because I have done so in another place,[1] but this book would lack completeness in greater measure than it does already if the subject were entirely passed by.

I well remember conducting a mission at the University of Leeds. After each session there was an opportunity for private conversations. A girl who was about to take her final degree examination said something like this : " When I get back home I know that the hardest thing in my religious life will be to stick the services in our little village chapel." She added things about that service which, in view of the preceding chapter, I need not relate. " So," she

[1] " Jesus and Ourselves," p. 109ff., *Jesus and the Way to God through Nature.*

233

added, " I think I shall simply go up
to the hills or into the woods. I shall
more easily find God there." Of course
I told her that would never do as a rule.
God ceases so soon to be real when we
evade men, especially fellow-seekers, and
seek Him selfishly for ourselves,[1] and I
reminded her of Him who was in the
Synagogue on the Sabbath day, *" as
His custom was."*[2] I reminded her that
He must have had to listen to some
pretty poor stuff from those old Rabbis,
but that if others lifted their heads during
the prayers and saw His face they would
come again ; that in any case when
He was there it would be easier to pray ;
that she had something to *give* in a
service as well as to get, and that her
minister would break his heart if she
deserted him instead of helping him to
make the service what both wanted it to
become. Since that date the spiritual
life of that little village church has been

[1] cf. p. 103 ff.
[2] Luke iv, 16.

transformed and renewed, and it has overflowed to another village. The girl not only attended regularly, but started a group which has become the spiritual power house of the neighbourhood.

At the same time many people do feel like that. And the Churches suffer and the people themselves lose *something* because they are looking for God in the woods.

Let us first of all admit the value of Nature as an aid in a search for God. How foolish he would be who sought to prove that a hush, which is of God, did not sometimes fall upon the spirit when we watch the sun set over the sea in some quiet place or wander in meditative mood among the silent lonely hills.

I can sit back in my chair now and get a sense of peace, a sense of spiritual inspiration, merely by letting pictures of the loveliness of Nature float in front of my mind. The sea beating in splendid fury at the base of cliffs ; the moors

silent in the haze of a summer afternoon
with only the sound of bees among
the wild thyme or a sheep-bell in the
distance; the mountains lifting huge
granite shoulders toward the sky till
the clouds kiss them as they pass; a
fruit tree in the orchard at springtime
covered with the glory of blossom;
the fens at sunset with the vast sky
over-arching all, the yellow sunset light
reflected in distant pools among the
rushes; a field of buttercups laughing
in the sunlight on a June morning;
a bowl of red roses in the firelight of a
quiet room; the abandoned trill of a
lark far up in the heavens; the white
glint of moonlit waves out at sea . . .

But I wonder what such pictures
would mean to me if I were in deep
trouble? What would they mean to
me if I had no other contacts with
God, if I had never been taught to link
the thought of God's loveliness with
them? If I were told that my dearest
had some incurable disease, would God

speak to me in the waves of the sea ? Or would those very waves mock me with heartless laughter ? If death snatched my little daughter what would the silent mountains say to me of comfort ? And if, in either case, I found help there, could I sincerely say to a heathen African who suffered thus, " The sea will whisper peace. The mountains will bring you comfort " ?

Can he find God in Nature ? If so, why hasn't he done so ? Why is it that in parts of the world where Nature is loveliest man seems often furthest from the God and Father of our Lord Jesus Christ ? Why did a villager I know walk ten miles to tell his minister that he was dissatisfied and wanted to find God ? Why didn't he sit in his own field of buttercups ?

In a certain mood, bringing thoughts of God derived from other sources, men have found God in Nature ; but even poets like Wordsworth and lovers of Nature like Richard Jefferies will tell us that though Nature will pay a huge dividend to a faith invested in her, without faith first brought to her and invested in her, her returns are nil. "The sea saith 'It is not in me,'" and the seeker for God in Nature may, and often does, return in despair feeling "There is no one there."

Let me quote here a story told by Henry Van Dusen [1] of a young man who returned home after a somewhat long absence. "As his key turned the latch and he entered the front door, he was greeted by silence. He climbed slowly to the second-floor room where, day by day and year by year, he had been accustomed to be met by a familiar figure and a familiar voice of welcome. Everything in that room was precisely as he had expected to find it. There on the table were books and magazines piled in customary fashion. On the desk was a vase of flowers, its arrangement

[1] *The Plain Man Seeks for God*, Henry P. Van Dusen, p. 28 (Scribners).

suggesting fingers with a peculiarly
delicate touch. Each chair and ornament
was in its usual place. There was almost
a distinctive aroma in the room. In
one corner was the great armchair where
the figure habitually sat, and beside it
some needlework as though just laid down.
It was all exactly as he had expected.
Everything in that room, everything,
was a ' revelation ' of his mother. But
—the chair was empty ; there was no
hearty voice in greeting ; the figure
was not there. Something like that is
the contrast between a God ' revealed '
through nature and conscience, and a
God who wills to reveal himself, speaking
to men one by one."

Men and women will continue, of
course, to seek God in Nature. Those
who have first found Him elsewhere,
will continue to read into Nature what
they have found, and the glory of
Nature will increase their sense of the
God of Nature. Some, frankly, deceive
themselves. They want a pleasing

æstheticism, a vague sense of comfort which beauty gives. They are too selfish to share the world's burden or listen to the world's cry of pain, and the "lovely feelings" Nature and Art can give us are differentiated from true religious feeling and prove a mere form of soothing æstheticism in that they make us critical of our fellows and impatient of their less refined and sensitive natures, whereas real religious feeling always produces love for others. The consciences of some "Nature Lovers" are so systematically drugged by lies and compromise that they have almost ceased to function. Their indifference to the real God is all but complete. But you will see them sneaking off on a fine Sunday on foot or by car, and their excuse will be that they find God in Nature. Their very conversation judges them. They will rave about the beauties of Nature, but they never say they have found there a power over sin. Their experiences make thrilling conversation in the drawing-room, but those experiences do not transform their lives. Nor do those experiences lead them to help others to enter them, or lead them to share the burden of the world. Some are sincere, of course, but when I learn how some of them spend the day with Nature (!) I think it would be more honest to say that they enjoyed a jolly picnic in pleasant surroundings. If they think once of God it is a God who is a false mental image which they themselves have set up. And as Dr. Temple says, such an image can lead one as far astray as a false metal image. Wordsworth distinguishes those who look on Nature " as in the hour of thoughtless youth " and those who have *learned* to look on Nature,

> not as in the hour
> Of thoughtless youth ; but hearing often times
> The still sad music of humanity.

It is the part of some of us to listen to that sad music, not in Nature but from the lips of living men and women who

241

Q

suffer. And few people but ministers
and doctors know the amount of suffering
that goes on behind the brave eyes and
firm lips of " ordinary men and women."
Here is a young man possessed by wild
temptation, which, if yielded to, will
wreck his career and break his mother's
heart. Shall I send him to the seaside
or tell him of a Friend who sticketh
closer than a brother ? Here is an
oldish man who in the evening of life
just cannot forget a sin he committed a
score of years ago, cannot forgive
himself, cannot put the burden down.
Shall I send him to the woods or tell
him of One who forgives us and carries
our sins on His own heart ? In the
woods he is more likely to find Nature
" red in tooth and claw," or " careless
of the single life " than the Father who
" pitieth His children " and " bindeth
up the broken in heart." Here is a young
mother with two or three little children
making constant demands on her life.
Her man is unemployed. She needs

some antidote against irritability and spoilt temper. Shall I tell her to sit at her bedroom window and watch the silent clouds float slowly by ? Or shall I tell her of One who offers her an inner peace which can keep her calm amid the demands of her hectic life— of One who seeks to enter her life more and more fully and give her strength and guidance in her difficult lot. So one could go on. For myself, speaking from my little experience of fifteen years of talking to men and women in various kinds of trouble, I should say that man's greatest need is God, and the most important question in the world for him is the question that forms the title of this book. And the God he needs is the God who is like Jesus—the God who is most readily found in Jesus. His name shall be called Immanuel, for God is with us. And this poor, lowly thing called the human heart is too great to be satisfied with Nature—too great for anything but God.

PART III
HOW SHALL I KNOW
I HAVE FOUND HIM?

I WANT to begin this chapter with one word of reiterated caution about "feeling." In religious matters we seem particularly prone to take our spiritual temperature with the thermometer of feeling. If moments come to us when we *feel* very deeply moved, sometimes to the point of tears, or uplifted with a tremendous feeling of exhilaration, we are ready enough then to deduce the movement of the spirit of God in our own hearts. A good many people, if asked how they were sure of God, would answer, "I feel Him near me."

We must take great care not to disparage the value of feeling. It is unlikely that a man's first approach to God will be made without feeling, just as it is difficult to think of a man falling in love without feeling; and I, for one, should wish to affirm that those moments when a man feels moved to tears or lifted to the highest are certainly moments when God is sweeping through his nature and this fact is partly revealed in feeling.

At the same time it is necessary to say very definitely that feeling is not the only measure of the nearness of God. The mistake of supposing the opposite accounts for the errors we have already noted.

1. Some people, because they are easily moved, suppose that they have the richest kind of experience of God.

2. Other people, who never feel anything, discredit their own spiritual experience because they think feeling is the only test of validity. They say, "I never feel like that." Others again feel awed and moved, perhaps, on a Sunday night at the close of some restful service, and on Monday morning they *feel* that the sky is as grey as ever it was, that the glory of Sunday has passed

away, and they have a curious kind of suspicion that religion is a drug, the effect of which passes off. It is the same mistake. The mistake of supposing that feeling is the only test of our religious life.

It is not so. There are three parts of the personality, of which feeling is only one. The other two are what the psychologists call " intellection " and " conation," or in less technical terms, knowing and willing, and if, because of some religious impact, our mind has ideas of God, if it thinks in terms of the Kingdom, if it bursts into a new sea of thought, then, if I may put it like this, the thermometer of intellection is just as reliable as the thermometer of emotion to register our spiritual temperature. Further, if after some religious contact our will is made strong to endure, and the will of God becomes more consciously our will, then the degree to which our will becomes one with God's, is a measure of the degree to which we have found God. Putting it another way, the thermometer of conation is as reliable as intellection or emotion.

The man who feels that the impact of God on his personality, registered by feeling on Sunday night, has disappeared on Monday morning, because it is no longer registered in the same way, would find the proof of the reality of Sunday night's experience if on Monday morning someone attempted to make him do the wrong thing or challenged his faith. He would then find that, in terms of mind and will, there was just as strong a sense of God as that which on Sunday night was measurable in terms of feeling. We can see this by recalling the analogy between love and religion. A man who loves his wife very dearly is not always registering that love in feeling. Life cannot be one long honeymoon, and even on the pictures the maximum time for a kiss is thirteen seconds. Indeed, there may be times when an introspective newly-wed wonders whether his love is passing. Generally it is only because he is making the same mistake in regard to love which so many make in regard to religion. He is supposing that the only reliable thermometer with which to take the temperature of his love is that of feeling. But let someone attack his wife or attack her good name and instantly his feeling is aroused. It was there all the time although dormant.

Let me leave the point there, repeating the warning that feeling is not the only valid estimate of a real experience of God.

I now want to suggest several ways in which I think a man may answer for himself the question, " How shall I know I have found Him ? " If a man, by an act of imaginative faith, puts out the hand of his spirit to touch One who is " nearer to us than breathing, closer than hands and feet," and if he so soaks his mind in the thought of God's presence (or the presence of Christ, which brings us to the same end) and makes that sense of contact as continuous as possible, then I think he may expect to find that his contact with God has brought about four results.

Firstly, a changed reaction to life. None of us, unless we do not mingle at all in the life of our fellows, can fail to notice the disabled lives that are being lived round about us. Possibly many of us are troubled about the disablement in our own lives. The constant expressions that people use are indicative of the disharmony of their souls. People are " fed-up " or " bored," or at best " jogging along " or " might be worse." They are lying on the deck, being taken wherever the winds and currents of life like to take them, instead of being at the wheel, in charge of their own lives, masters of their fate and captains of their souls. Yet everyone—I think there are no exceptions to this—desires to be in charge of life, to have some sense of meaning and purpose, of peace and beauty in life. Now, there are some souls who are in charge of their own lives. The wheel is in their hands. They are not afraid of wind or tempest, rock or whirlpool. They feel there is Someone standing by their side, a Pilot with whom they are in constant touch, who gives them whatever direction they need. Their faces are radiant, their shoulders squared, the tang of the sea is pleasant to them, the morning breezes a tonic to them. They are alive as others are not alive ; strong when others hesitate and turn back. Their hearts are at rest, not because everything comes right, but because they believe that nothing can go wrong with such a Pilot on board. They have the sense that nothing matters as long as their relationship with their Pilot is close and deep and real. They have found God. They know it and they have a changed reaction to life. This changed reaction means at least three important things.

(*a*) A new sense of power. I do not mean the power of the unaided will. Christianity

would not be the good news it is, if it
merely told us to exert our wills. What
is offered is a will re-energised by the
power of God dwelling in us. Things
we thought impossible are now bravely
tackled. Temptations we thought we
should never conquer are—sometimes
slowly, sometimes quickly—overcome.
We have a new power over sin. We
begin to glimpse the power that could
make a mortal man cry out " In Him
that strengtheneth me, I am able for
anything."

(*b*) A new sense of peace. I do not
mean a peace secured by leaving the
field of life's battle in order to recover.[1]
I mean a peace *in* battle ; a peace, then,
not dependent on circumstances, but
gloriously independent of them. I mean
an inner serenity in the midst of turmoil
not gained because the diary is not full,
but gained because God keeps the heart
quiet. A peace which the world cannot
give and cannot take away—a peace

[1] cf. " O, for the wings of a dove," etc.

which belongs to the eternal silences. We begin to glimpse the serenity that could make a mortal man name all the things which so often destroy peace and then cry out, " *in* all these things,"—not by escape from them—" we are more than conquerors, through Him."

(*ι*) A new sense of joy. I do not mean a joy which comes from high spirits and good health, from having enough to live on, friends and home and all the blessings of this life. I do not even mean a joy which is the opposite of sorrow and grief and pain. I mean a joy that persists through all those things, though "joys be withered all and dead." A joy which is not caused by the absence of sorrows or killed by their presence ; a joy that can send us into the world of need and sorrow and pain instead of making us shrink from them, because in God we and the world have a remedy for them; a joy that shines even through our tears, and which comes from knowing that because we

255

are wholly His and in His capable hands He will bring us through to the goal of His purposes with honour and ultimate gain, and that all things will be made plain to those who go on loving. A joy that is no mere " bubbly " feeling, but a deep, quiet radiance ; a sentiment which is the abiding spring from which emotional joy does sometimes bubble forth. We shall glimpse then the joy that could make that same mortal man name the perils and losses and sufferings he had sustained and cry out in triumph that " All things work together for good to them that love God."

Secondly, a changed motive in daily work. Here is a girl whose job it is to help in a chocolate factory. I have seen such girls at work. The wage is low, the room is stuffy, the work is monotonous, the forewoman is cantankerous. For long months, even years, the girl feels a victim of drudgery. She finds that she needs " the pictures " three times a week to make life possible.

She is "fed-up." There is resentment, bitterness, something of hatred in her heart. Suddenly something happens—her tired, restless spirit is thrown back on God. In some quiet place her spirit puts out its trembling hands to touch Someone. It seems to her as if a brave, strong hand clasps her own, gives her a sense of otherness—a sense that life can never be lonely any more. She goes back to her factory next morning a different girl. Those who know best are quick to feel that something has happened. There is a quiet strength about her, a sense of inward peace, a radiant happiness in her face. But it is more than a changed reaction to life; it is a changed reaction to her work. She feels that she is not working for the boss any longer;[1] not working to escape the censure of a forewoman. God is in the factory; it is holy ground; she is working for Him now and in His presence. She believes, what is certainly

[1] See Ephes. vi, 6-7.

R

true, that He takes an interest in the
making of chocolates, that He is glad
when the whirl which she makes on the
top of them comes out just as it should,
when the required number just fit into
the box. If He is interested in the
sparrow's life and doings, if He is
interested in the hair of her head, He is
interested in the work of her fingers
as she makes her living. There is a
new attitude to work, an attitude capable
of making all jobs sacred, since no one's
work is sacred through the nature of
the work, but through the nature of the
spirit brought to the work; and she is
making chocolates now to the glory of
God in as true a sense as some of us
try to make sermons.

Thirdly, a changed attitude to men
and women. There are a few people
—not very many it must be confessed
—who really do love their fellows,
who are not suspicious of them, who,
while not so blind that they cannot
see the weak points in other people,

yet believe passionately in their best, and act to their fellows always in such a way as to draw that best forth. I think that is what Jesus means by loving one another. It is hard to make oneself love, and sometimes we are tempted to turn round even on the words of Christ and say, " I cannot love my fellows because I am commanded to. Love is a spontaneous thing or not love, and it cannot be spontaneous unless my brother shows himself to be lovable." Christ's answer is that everyone is lovable if he is looked at in the right way, and that it is our duty so to look. There are some spirits who always look at their fellows like that, who honestly and sincerely, without jealousy, rejoice in the success of other people, and who truly grieve in the mistakes of other people. They are the people who have found God. They have a concern for their fellows, which is not found in either the fussing of the philanthropist or the indifference of the worldling, but a love and belief and desire which would fain draw all men into that new world which Christ offers and which they themselves have found. The New Testament has a special word for this attitude, " agapé." It is not just being kind and generous, for St. Paul says, " If I give all my goods to feed the poor and have not agapé it counts for nothing." It is an outgoing love to all—the critic, the enemy, the difficult, the " impossible " people; a love which springs from the sense that God loves us and all men alike; from the sense that in His mercy He has forgiven us and brought us home; from the desire that all the world should taste and see the riches of His grace, since " the arms of love that compass me, would all mankind embrace." How shall I know I have found Him ? " We *know* that we have passed from death unto life," says St. John, " *because we love the brethren*."[1]

Fourthly, a desire to commune with

[1] 1 John iii, 14.

Him. I think we ought to speak carefully here. I do not mean that an occasional mood in which we do not desire Him is a sign that we have never had any contact with Him. There are sometimes physical causes capable, apparently, of clouding our faith. There are occasional turnings back which it would be cruel to suggest invalidate all our experiences of God. If a child is naughty and rebellious for half an hour, it is not a disparagement of all his previous communion with his father ; and it is the same with us and our Heavenly Father. Moreover, the whole question of keeping our communion with God needs going into more fully than we can compass here. But if we have found God in the sense in which the New Testament offers Him to us in Christ, I am sure that we shall have seen enough to want more. We shall never be *content* again in the far country. We shall never be quite the same again. Some of us keep on slipping back into old habits, doing and saying things for which we hate ourselves; but in His infinite mercy He is always willing to receive us back again, urges us to start again in His strength instead of our own; and for our part we do at least know where serenity and power are to be found, and after a time—when the hollowness of worldliness has smitten us again—we shall turn to Him again because only in Him have we ever found reality, only in Him have we found satisfaction, only in Him have we found the truest life of our best selves. We may turn aside into the jungles beside the path, because some poisonous flower blooms there which the world praises and tells us to possess, or because some adventure allures us by its base appeal. But if we have found God we know the path back again, and torn, and bitten, and stung we shall tread it again, for we know it is the only path which can bring us out where, in our best moments, we want to be. So, though it may mean at first a hundred new starts a week, we shall proceed with the process of being saved,[1] realising that the only ultimate tragedy would be not to start again, and thus not only disbelieve in ourselves but disbelieve in His power to save us. And the process will lead to the complete surrender of ourselves to Him—to the surrender of things which we don't yet see as sin—until the soul, at last, finds its greatest liberty and joy in doing His will, finds also how much more there is still to find, and in Him lives and moves and has its being. " To be saved," said a member of my Friday Fellowship, " is to want God always." I think it would not be easy to improve that definition.

But we must not say, " My life shows none of these changed reactions or those deep desires, and therefore my experience of God is an illusion." Is

[1] Acts ii, 47 : " The Lord added to them day by day those that were being saved."

263

not the answer that we must keep on putting out our hand to touch Him, repeating act upon act of imaginative faith, beginning again with God, day after day, if necessary, believing that He wants us more than we want Him, believes in us more than we believe in Him, loves us more than we shall ever love Him, and that to give up our quest is to deprive Him, to deprive ourselves, and to allow ourselves to sink into the rut of compromise which is the grave of so much splendid character?

Men who walked with Jesus were not changed in the twinkling of an eye. The tracks of habit in their minds were too deep. Doubts and fears continually assailed them; old passions swept through them. But they kept turning back to Him; they put out their hands and touched His friendship. They knew that in His friendship they had found God. They sometimes turned their backs on their experience and fell into sin. But,

even so, life could never be the same
again, for they knew where strength
and radiance and peace werc to be found.
Gradually the spell of His life deepened.
Area after area in their nature was
conquered until they became like Him,
shared His reaction to life, shared His
great, patient love for men.

We know that if He were here in
the flesh, through Him we should find
it easy to find God. Let us by an
act of imaginative faith realise that
even at this moment He stands up
in our midst, offering us His precious
friendship and its gracious fruits. We
cannot see His face or hear that beloved
voice ; but men, by faith, have taken
Him at His word and found God as
truly as men did who followed Him in
Galilee so long ago. Indeed, even to
think of Him opens floodgates of energy
and peace within the soul. All through
the ages since He ascended, men and
women, irrespective of culture or " temperament," have found God in Jesus.

They know it is God they have found, for no one else could do such mighty works in them. No one else has such an effect on my life as He. No contact with any other personality living or dead has the effect on me which He has. They tend to push me into inferiority. But He, infinitely greater, makes me believe in myself. I am humbled utterly, but as utterly exalted. " The endeavour to make Jesus actual has the striking effect that for anyone adventurous enough to make a spiritual experiment He becomes the most stimulating creative Comrade any man could have."[1]

To find Jesus means that I hate sin with a new hatred, that so far from being critical I want to worship, that while I hate myself I am not driven, as other historical figures drive me, into inferiority. I believe in myself, am delivered from myself, am admitted into a new kingdom of creative values, am

[1] W. Kirkland, *Who is this Jesus?* p. 17.

delivered even from my principles and resolutions and pledges and the other railings I have put up on the side of the road to keep myself straight. I find myself pushing the railings over. I am on the moors, laughing and running, throwing up my hat. I am free and life is intoxicating. I find the glory of the liberty of the sons of God. I am delivered from all the cares of selfhood into the free country of otherness, and I tend to become as impatient of railings and roads and signposts as a man who is in love with his wife would be impatient of written promises and pledges that he would stand by her always. Love is the country of freedom, and to find Christ is to be free from self and from every bond save love.

Who seeketh finds : what shall be his relief
Who hath no power to seek, no heart to pray,
No sense of God ? . . . .
Be still, sad soul ! Lift thou no passionate cry,
    But spread the desert of thy being bare
To the full searching of the All-seeing eye :

HOW CAN I FIND GOD?

Wait—and through dark misgiving, blank despair,
God will come down in pity, and fill the dry
Dead place with light, and life, and vernal air.[1]

[1] J. C. Shairp, *Poems*.

EPILOGUE

MY last word must leave the emphasis in the right place. How can *I* find God? The title stands, but my book has been an attempt to show how that *I* can be got out of the way so that God can find us.

"If I seek Him, I have not far to go. For it is not the sheep that finds the Shepherd. The Shepherd finds the sheep. His journey is begun before mine. 'Behold I stand at the door and knock' we read; and all our 'seeking,' which seems to us so arduous, is only our half-reluctant rising to open the door. We are disturbed because He is near. We only come because He calls. And if at last we love, it is because He first loved us and came near enough to make it known.

"If I come, He cannot refuse me. He

271

cannot deny Himself; He cannot deny His Cross; He will not unsay what He has said or undo what He has done. We cannot conceive of Jesus in the days of His flesh shutting His door against anyone who came for help. And He is the same yesterday, to-day, and for ever. He will not refuse me. But this is still too poor a word. He will welcome, and in that welcome all things are given—utter forgiveness first of all . . .

"And the one true response is to trust Him to do what He is pledged to do—to do a Saviour's work, to do it now and to do it always. It is He Himself who is presented to us. We may ignore Him or respond to Him. Or, fearing an encounter, we may postpone our response, thinking perhaps to learn more about it, to answer some further questions, to amend and tidy our lives, so as to be more ready for it; but this is deceiving ourselves and avoiding Him. But when we do respond and consent to be won just as we are, then, in our Lord's word, ' Salvation has come to this house ! ' "[1]

No words of mine could better express that emphasis which I would leave as the final impression in the reader's mind. This encounter with God is one towards which He presses us with every means He can use, save those which would deny His nature or ours. That gentle but persistent, and one might say inexorable, pressure is what, on our side, we call our search for Him, and that pressure will continue this side of the grave and the other until we have become all that He can make us. If we are wise the emphasis will be always on Him. Our search is His progressive finding of us. Without Him we could not seek Him and when we find Him, and are brought into a filial relation with Him through the forgiveness of our sins, then He begins a work in us which is

---

[1] *Christ, the Saviour of Man*, pp. 8-10. W. R. Maltby, Sheffield Congress Booklets (Epworth Press), 1d.

S

the work of His grace and not the result of our new effort or resolution.

The case of St. Paul is surely convincing. If man could be changed by any effort of his own surely St. Paul with his first-class brains, his intuitive insight, his indomitable will, his untiring devotion, his magnificent energy, would have stood a good chance. But listen— " I cannot understand my own actions : I do not act as I want to act ; on the contrary, I do what I detest . . . the wish is there, but not the power of doing what is right. I cannot be good as I want to be, and I do wrong against my wishes. . . . Miserable wretch that I am ! Who will rescue me from this body of death ? God will ! Thanks be to Him through Jesus Christ our Lord ! "[1]

God will do it ! " Apart from Me," says Jesus according to the fourth Evangelist, " ye can do nothing." " In Him that strengtheneth me," says St.

[1] Rom. vii, 15ff. (Moffatt).

Paul, "I can do anything." What could be greater than that tremendous contrast between "nothing" and "anything." And the New Testament is a gospel, it is good news, just because it is not the laying of an even greater burden on the will and whipping it to some greater effort, but the re-energising of the will by the power of a transforming Christ working in us. The difference is that of trying to make a briar produce beautiful roses by any conceivable treatment from without, and grafting into it that which will change from within and send through the secret recesses of the rose's hidden life the glory which can never otherwise be revealed. "I am the Vine, ye are the branches," He says; "Abide in Me and I in you. As a branch cannot bear fruit of itself except it abide in the vine, so neither can ye except ye abide in Me."[1]

Some may say, what is quite true, that

[1] John xv, 4-5

the will must be exercised. But I am pleading, with a conviction based on my own past failures as well as the honoured confidence of others, that the only way we can live the life we were made to live and make God's dreams come true in us is to surrender our lives to Him and just daily and, if need be, hourly rely on His power—" to come to God," as Du Bose puts it, " not waiting to be good, and to find *in Him* all that we need for righteousness."

" But are we not told to strive to enter the narrow way ? " Yes, but He says 'I am the Way.' " Are we not taught to fight the good fight ? " No, we are taught to 'fight the good fight *of faith*,[1] and to *lay hold* on eternal life.' The battle is with our doubts that something is being offered. " Are we not taught to put on the armour of God ? "[2] Yes, but the only weapon is 'the sword *of the Spirit*.' " Be strong

[1] I Tim. vi, 12.
[2] Ephes. vi, 11.

in the Lord and in the power of His might."[1] And that is a *gift*, the free gift of God which God is as ready to give as a father is ready to give food to his child. Indeed " how much more shall your Heavenly Father give the Holy Spirit to them that ask Him." [2]

What missionary would consent to go abroad to tell a people who knew not God to " try harder " ? He goes, with a radiant experience which has changed him, to offer a gift—the gift of a friendship that can change any man and bring him pardon first, and then power and peace and joy and outgoing love for others, whatever poor little bit of will-power he happens to have.

When I was in India I once conceived the ambition of being a singer. If I had been married then, this conceit would have been strangled at birth. But it so took hold of me that I bought several songs and murdered them. One

[1] Ephes. vi, 10.
[2] Luke xi. 13. See *The Transforming Friendship* for the further working out of this important theme.

evening I invited a real musician to dinner and suggested to him that he should play my accompaniments. He looked up with surprise. " I didn't know you sang," said he, looking at me with kindly eyes, little knowing what was in store for him. Then I started. I can see him now trying so hard to be polite. But at last his head was in his hands lest I should see the agony in his face. " Do you think I had better have lessons ? " said I. " No, I don't think I would," he said gently. I didn't. I have never sung alone since then, except in the bathroom. I knew it was beyond me, and he did, too. Yes, even if I practised for ever.

If only he could have imparted *himself* to me : he who tingled with music to his finger tips. Then, though I should have needed to practise I should have *begun* to enter a new world that is all but closed to me.

This is what Christ offers—the gift of Himself imparted to me. " I live," said St. Paul, struggling with the amazing thing that had happened, "I am still Paul, but a new Paul, released from old inhibitions and the power of old sins, gloriously free from fear, enabled for every situation." His spirit was shouting songs of joy, his soul bathed in ineffable peace, his whole being bursting to pass on this amazing experience. "I live and yet no longer I, but *Christ liveth in me*,[1] and that life which I now live in the flesh I live by faith in the Son of God, who loved me and gave Himself up for me."

There is a story in the life of Charles Wesley relevant here.[2] After Charles Wesley had preached on the new life in Christ which is offered, an Anglican clergyman came up to him and said, "That is what I want. I must seek it by a long course of devotional discipline, by years given to reading the Bible and years devoted to prayer." Fortunately

---

[1] Gal. ii, 20.

[2] I owe it to my friend, Rev. Prof. J. Arundel Chapman. See his excellent pamphlet "God's Free Offer," Fellowship of the Kingdom Pamphlets. (Epworth Press).

for us all he was wrong, and Charles Wesley did not fail to tell him so. We cannot deserve God. We can only accept Him. All that we seek from Him—pardon, power, peace and joy—we cannot merit. We can only receive. These things are not of ourselves. They are the gift of God. Because they are gifts they are not to be fought for or even understood, but received. If God did not give them we could not get them. If He gives them we have only to take them.

So I cannot close by asking you to make a new resolution or to try harder. I close by asking you to make an act of entire surrender of yourself to God; to accept His pardon and grace; to give Him a chance, by daily communion and quiet meditation, to indwell you more and more fully so that His power may fire your will, defeat the power of temptation, banish your fears, keep your heart quiet and serene and joyous and loving. I close by asking you to join a fellowship of others who are seeking, finding, and for ever seeking more; to submit to the surgery of confession to God, and, if that does not give you release, to confess to men; to begin this new life again now with God as daily Guide; to make any restitution which may be necessary and possible and right; and immediately to set about telling the good news to someone else that he or she also may find the greatest thing in the world.

Tell God that you can't go on any longer as you are; that you are at the end of your tether and at sixes and sevens with yourself and everyone else. Tell Him you don't know what you do believe, and that you have no will power left and that you can't pray. Tell Him you've broken most of the good resolutions you ever made and you haven't the heart to make more. Tell Him that you are not always quite honest, often selfish, unloving and impure. And then ask Him if He can do anything with you.

I know what He will say. "He that cometh to Me I will in no wise cast out."

> If I ask Him to receive me,
> Will He say me nay ?
> Not till earth and not till heaven
> Pass away.

And if we are honest and sincere and stop bothering about our feelings ; if only we will loose our hold on self and not hide from Him, or be too proud to let Him forgive us, or defend ourselves against Him, He will change us. "What fools we are," said a friend of mine recently ; "we cling to ourselves as drowning men cling to the very last plank of a broken ship on the ocean— and it is the ocean that bears us ! " We will stupidly trust in ourselves, and worry about *our* feelings, *our* pride and what people will think of *us*. Let us throw ourselves on His grace !

> Let me no more my comfort draw
> From my frail hold on Thee.
> Only in this rejoice with awe,
> *Thy mighty grasp of me.*

QUESTIONARY

Prologue.

1. What would you say to a person who says, " I do not want to find God. I get on quite well without bothering about religion " ?
2. What would you say to a person who says, " I only want God when I am unhappy and it seems so mean just to seek Him then that I never pray " ?
3. If Jesus in the flesh met with you and talked to you, what do you think He would say first ?
4. Does anyone live without conscious compromise in the modern world ? What happens ?
5. If the Christians in the early Church had been like you, how far would Christianity have spread ?

PART I.

Chapter I.

1. What would you say to a man who says he wants to repent but cannot ?
2. Distinguish between self-pity and repentance.
3. Discuss the place of feeling in repentance.
4. Jesus said, " Repent and believe " (Mark i, 15). If someone had asked, " How ? ", what do you think He would have said ?

Chapter II.

1. Discuss the place of the intellectual acceptance of doctrine in the life of the Christian.
2. What would be the attitude of Jesus to our intellectual problems ?
3. Is intellectual doubt ever a barrier to true Christian living ?
4. Does it matter what a man believes ?
5. Make a list of what you imagine were the intellectual beliefs of Peter,
   (*a*) The night Jesus was crucified,
   (*b*) The night after Pentecost.
6. Do men really hide behind intellectual doubts ?

Chapter III.

1. John Smith says he believes that all that God requires is that a man should live a decent life and be kind to others. Do you agree ?
2. Are some people feverishly engaging in " service " so that they may not stop to let God find them ?
   Have you got an experience of God which makes others long to have it ?
4. Are the " radiant face " and " infectious gaiety " matters of temperament ?
5. Does the Church evade the challenge of Christ by offering Him good work and faithful service ?
6. What is the first work of the Christian Church ? What of yours ? What are you doing about it ?

Chapter IV.

1. " We can be so inoculated by small doses of Christianity that we can't catch the big thing." Discuss this.

2. How can we get the impression of the New Testament writings which they made on the minds of those who heard them for the first time ?
3. " The conventional churchman is the hardest in the world to win." Discuss this.
4. Discuss the " violence " of Jesus. Are we justified in being violent with those we seek to help ? Under what conditions ?

Chapter V.
1. " Religion is dope." Discuss this. Is it sometimes true ?
2. Was the Psalmist wrong in likening God to a " Shield " ?
3. Did the comforting words of Christ all contain challenges ? Instances, please.
4. Does religion ever mean escape from calamity ?

Chapter VI.
1. What is forgiveness ?
2. What would you say to a man who found it hard to forgive another an injury done to one dearly loved ?
3. " Time heals all things." Discuss this.
4. Why did Jesus put that conditional clause in the Lord's Prayer ?
5. What should condition our escape from the demands of life ?

Chapter VII.
1. Name some common rationalisations made by Christians.

2. Discuss ways in which we can find the doors we have shut against God.
3. Why have religious people got the name of being " spoil sports," " wet blankets," " long faced," and so on?
4. Name some criticisms which are expressions of inverted envy.

PART II.

Chapter I.

1. Discuss the definition of "finding God," on page 145.
2. What is the place of emotion in a religious experience? Is it legitimate for the preacher to make emotional appeals?
3. "I pray but I don't feel any different." Discuss this.
4. Does love ever fail to triumph?

Chapter II.

1. Might a man, by following the advice on pages 166-169, delude himself? What are the tests?
2. If someone asked you how he might find God, would you say, " Read this——" or " Hear so and so," or could you tell him out of your own experience?
3. How is a man to " put the emphasis on God's friendship "? Be practical.
4. " A heart lifted up in adoration and a will bent to daily obedience will not go unrewarded." Discuss this.

QUESTIONARY

Chapter III.

1. Are there folk who are spending themselves in unselfish service for others and yet who have no religious experience or any desire for God ? Is there such a thing as unconscious religion ?
2. What are the essentials of missionary candidature ?
3. Would you say to a young seeker, " You must not do any more Christian service or Church work until you have found God ?
4. Some service is an expression of religion and some is an evasion of religion. Discuss this.

Chapter IV.

1. Can a man be a Christian and never go to church ?
2. Answer a man who says, " Services bore me. I could never find God that way."
3. Discuss the criticisms on pages 209-217 (Anglican Service).
4. Should the Church restate her creeds in modern language ?
5. Discuss the criticisms on pages 217-223 (Free Church Service).
6. Discuss the place of sacraments in Christian worship.

Chapter V.

1. Under what conditions in ourselves does God speak to us in Nature ?
2. Does contact with Nature ever inspire man to sacrificial service ?

3. Distinguish between æsthetic and religious feelings aroused by Nature.

PART III.

1. Can a man find God without possessing new power, or peace, or joy ?
2. " A good deal of alleged Christian joy is sheer health and high spirits." Discuss this.
3. Is God really interested in the details of our lives ? But what is a detail ?
4. " Being saved is to want God always." Discuss this.

Epilogue.

1. Discuss the place of the will in the Christian life.
2. Is the advice of the New Testament, " Try harder," or " Believe differently " ?
3. What did our Lord mean by His words that of all men born of women there had never arisen a greater than John the Baptist, " nevertheless he that is least in the Kingdom of Heaven is greater than he."
4. Does the New Testament offer an experience utterly different in kind from that of trying to live a good moral life ? What is the difference ?

288